Harry S. Truman

33rd President of
the United States

A photographic portrait of Harry Truman that was taken while he was serving as 33rd President of the United States. (Library of Congress.)

Harry S. Truman
33rd President of the United States

David R. Collins

 Garrett Educational Corporation

Manufactured in the United States of America

Edited and produced by Synthegraphics Corporation

Library of Congress Cataloging in Publication Data

Collins, David R.
  Harry S. Truman, 33rd President of the United States.

  (Presidents of the United States)
  Bibliography: p.
  Includes index.
  Summary: Focuses on the personality, early life, family, career, and significant contributions of President Truman.
  1. Truman, Harry S., 1884–1972 – Juvenile literature.
2. Presidents – United States – Biography – Juvenile literature. [1. Truman, Harry S., 1884–1972.
2. Presidents] I. Title. II. Series.
E814.C63 1988   973.918′092′4 [B] [92]   87-32750
ISBN 0-944483-00-3

Contents

Chronology for Harry S. Truman

1884 Born on May 8

1901 Graduated from Independence (Missouri) High School

1917–1919 Served in United States Army

1919 Married Bess Elizabeth Wallace, June 28

1919–1921 Worked as a partner in haberdashery business

1922 Elected county judge

1935–1944 Served as United States senator from Missouri

1944 Elected Vice-President under Franklin D. Roosevelt

1945 Sworn in as 33rd President on April 12 after Roosevelt dies

1945 Signed United Nations Charter, June 26

1947 Introduced Truman Doctrine

1948 Introduced Marshall Plan

1948 Elected President

1950 Korean conflict began

1953 Returned to Independence, Missouri

1972 Died on December 26

Chapter 1
An End and a Beginning

April 12, 1945. It was finally coming to an end. Those agonizing years of World War II that had turned the United States into a mighty military machine were drawing to a close.

Even leaders of the United States government had turned their attention to other matters. On the floor of the Senate, Senator Alexander Wiley of Wisconsin was expounding on water rights related to a forthcoming treaty with Mexico. His lengthy oration had gathered few listeners. Usually Senate President Harry S. Truman forced himself to center his attention on the speech being given, but this afternoon he found Wiley especially windy and unfamiliar with the subject. Truman dashed off a letter to his mother and sister back home in Independence, Missouri, then headed to the office of Speaker of the House Sam Rayburn. Such meetings always promised jovial conversation, accompanied with bourbon and tap water.

There would be no talk and drinks on this particular Thursday, however. Told by Rayburn to call the White House, Truman complied. He was then told by Steve Early, press secretary to President Franklin Roosevelt, to come right over. Excusing himself, Truman took the underground corridors to his Senate office, informed his secretary where he was going, headed to his car, and was chauffeured to his destination.

There was little time to speculate about the reason to come to the White House. It was not Truman's nature to do so anyway. As a former military man, he had learned to take orders without question—a talent he used even more as the Vice-President. No, Truman did not suspect there was anything amiss. Perhaps President Roosevelt had returned from a short vacation trip to Warm Springs, Georgia, to attend the funeral of his friend Bishop Atwood. Maybe there was something special the President wanted done.

Reaching the White House, Truman was ushered to Mrs. Roosevelt's second-floor study. The bespectacled Vice-President glanced around the room, then faced a woman whose eyes looked sad and weary. Eleanor Roosevelt gently placed her hand on Truman's shoulder. "Harry," she said, "the President is dead."

The words struck like a physical blow to the body. President Roosevelt dead? Of course, he had not looked well lately, not been his usual and robust self. But dead? Truman's eyes met those in front of him. "Is there anything I can do for you?" he asked. Mrs. Roosevelt shook her head. "Is there anything *we* can do for you?" she whispered. "For you are the one in trouble now."

For the second time, the reality of Mrs. Roosevelt's words stunned Harry Truman. Yes, he was in charge now. A friend, a good friend, was gone, but he had been much more than just a good friend. He had been a leader. Now those reins of leadership had passed into Truman's hands.

If anyone understood the inner workings of American political power, it was Harry S. Truman. He had spent a lifetime studying the nation's history and operating within the mainstream of governmental service. Now, everything he knew was about to be tested. He immediately called his home, summoning his wife Bess and daughter Margaret to the White House. The Chief Justice of the Supreme Court was sent for to administer the oath of office, while additional calls went out to convene Cabinet members and government officials. At exactly 7:09 P.M. on April 12, 1945, Harry S. Truman took the oath of office and became the 33rd President of the United States. Ironically, only the day before, he had told a press conference how much he enjoyed serving in the Senate. "It's the greatest place on earth," he had said. But all of that was in the past now. It had become a part of the personal history of Harry S. Truman, mingling with the days and years of long ago in Missouri.

MISSOURI ROOTS

The President's home at 1600 Pennsylvania Avenue in Washington, D.C., was a far cry from the plain and unnumbered white frame house in Lamar, Missouri, where John and Martha Truman welcomed their first child on May 8, 1884. A short man, called "Peanuts" by his friends, John Truman accepted the news of a son being born with little more than a stoic nod, yet within 24 hours he was hanging a horseshoe above the front door of the house. "Just to bring the boy luck!" he yelled to his neighbors.

In contrast to her husband's serious nature, which most people attributed to a reserved British ancestry, Martha Truman was always ready to share a laugh at any moment and for the slightest reason. Her own family background was German, from which she claimed to have inherited her stubbornness, but it was well hidden beneath a manner which reflected a genuine concern for family and friends as well as a total desire to be useful. A skilled horseback rider, she was a tremendous asset to her husband's mule-trading business, causing people to remark, "What John Truman doesn't know about a horse or a mule, his missus does." The doors of their white frame house were always open to friends and relatives who gathered to talk about topics ranging from pol-

From a white house in Lamar, Missouri, to the White House in Washington, D.C.—few people would have guessed that the baby born on May 8, 1884, in this modest home would one day reside in the home of the Presidents. (Harry S. Truman Library.)

itics to tales of the days when famed lawman Wyatt Earp served as constable of Lamar.

Averting a Family Feud

The new addition to the Truman family provided considerable controversy when the selection of an appropriate name threatened to cause major problems. No one questioned the right of the new parents to supply the first name—Harrison, or Harry for short; it was the middle name that caused tension. It was assumed by those on John Truman's side of the family that the new baby would be christened Harrison Shippe Truman, taking his middle name from his paternal grandfather. Those on Martha's side of the family were equally convinced that the boy should be called Harrison Solomon Truman, after the baby's maternal grandfather. Wisely, the parents compromised and had the boy christened Harrison S. Truman, the middle initial standing for Shippe or Solomon, depending on whom you spoke to in the family.

Despite his reputation as an honest animal trader, John Truman could not keep a healthy business going in Lamar. He moved his family to nearby Harrisonville, where a second son, John Vivian, was born in April of 1886. However, finances did not improve with the move to Harrisonville, so the Truman family next went to Grandview, where they moved in with Martha's parents. With 600 acres to help farm, John gave up his business as a horse and mule trader.

In August of 1889, another baby was welcomed into the Truman family. This one a daughter, she was promptly christened Mary Jane. Then, with the death of Martha's father, John decided to sell the Grandview farm and return to animal trading, which he had sorely missed. But this time the family headed to a big city.

Martha Ellen Young Truman and John Anderson Truman,
Harry's parents, posed for this wedding portrait in 1882.
(Harry S. Truman Library.)

Growing Up in Independence

Independence, Missouri, boasted a population of 6,000 residents in 1890 and a colorful history as well. For pioneers traveling west on the Santa Fe and Oregon Trails, the town was a final stopping point before braving the wilderness beyond. Jesse James, the notorious outlaw, and his gang used the town as a hideout after the end of the Civil War in 1865. Mormon leader Joseph Smith had come to Independence hoping to make it a stronghold for his faithful religious following. But the residents had little use for Mormon thinking, which allowed a man to have more than one wife, and Smith was run out of town. No one loved listening to such stories of Independence more than young Harry Truman, who sat for hours enjoying the conversation of his parents and their visitors.

John Truman often allowed his son to join him as he worked trading horses and mules, but Harry was admonished not to carry everything said home. "Horse tradin' is man's work that demands man's language," John Truman declared. "Just don't be telling your mother every word you hear. Some words are for men and others are for ladies. You understand, son?" "Sure," Harry lied.

But if Harry picked up a hearty supply of crusty "mentalk" being with his father, the boy learned a great deal more than language by being with his mother. Although Martha Truman was in no hurry to send Harry off to school, she took an early interest in his education. By the time he was five, Harry could read with speed and precision, figure number problems in his head, follow complicated directions, and write the alphabet with a strong, sure hand.

"Flat Eyeballs"

Harry's quick mind and his desire to learn helped to hide a problem that finally came to light shortly before he went off

Four-year-old Harry Truman and his brother, two-year-old Vivian, display the latest in young boys' fashions in 1888. (Harry S. Truman Library.)

to school. The Truman family had returned to Grandview for a special Fourth of July celebration. As an enraptured audience on the ground squealed with delight at the sight of exploding fireworks in the sky, Martha Truman noticed that her older son seldom looked up. She then remembered other times when he failed to notice people or animals in the distance. Yet the boy read the Bible so easily without ever missing a word.

As soon as she could, Martha Truman took Harry to an eye doctor in Kansas City, where her suspicions were confirmed. Harry was diagnosed as having "flat eyeballs," a vision problem which made it impossible for him to recognize objects at a distance. Few children were ever prescribed glasses at that time, but Martha Truman insisted, and Harry was soon fitted with thick-lensed glasses and warned to avoid any activity that might break them.

The sacrifice was not as big for Harry as it might have been for other boys, because now he could read all he wished, and books always offered him special worlds of action and adventure. He also countered his visual problem with resourcefulness by securing his own spot when the boys gathered for a game of baseball. "I'll be the umpire!" the bespectacled boy would declare with a tone that no one would challenge, and Harry managed to remain a vital part of the fun without having contact or risking damage to his glasses.

"Little Sissy Truman!"

Despite his efforts to be a part of the gang, Harry discovered there were those who did not appreciate an undersized boy with oversized glasses. Anyone who spent as much time as he did with his face buried inside the pages of books was regarded with suspicion, even contempt, by those who considered themselves the tough members of the Independence community. "Sissy" was the name he heard more than once.

"Little sissy Truman!" The name hurt. It had to. But Harry gritted his teeth and refused to be drawn into an open fight. Often he recalled his mother's words, "Fighting is for babies," which helped him turn away from physical encounters.

Harry would resist the urge to blacken an eye or bloody a nose. Instead, he would simply grab his books and head for the Independence Public Library. Biographies, especially the lives of great generals, and famous historical events were his favorite readings. He memorized countless facts and figures for sharing at the supper table or in the classroom. A master of trivia, the quickness with which he collected information, analyzed causes and effects, and evaluated overall outcomes provided a discipline for his mind which proved a valuable asset later in life.

Harry also enjoyed listening to his mother play the piano and jumped at the chance to take lessons when she suggested it. Once again he ignored the taunts and jeers of those who thought music lessons were just for sissies, listening only to the sounds he made as his hands flew gracefully over the piano keyboard.

Harry's bond with his mother deepened even further when a severe bout of diphtheria paralyzed his arms and legs. He spent seven months at home, watching his mother cook, sew, and clean. Outdoor outings were only possible when his father would lift the boy up and wheel him around the neighborhood in a baby buggy. Slowly Harry recovered, due largely to his father and mother building his confidence while exercising his body each day. "He's a fighter!" a proud John Truman told everyone, once his son regained his health.

FIRST TASTE OF POLITICS

The presidential campaign of 1892 caused a political fever that infected cities and towns across the nation. John Truman made no secret of his support for the Democratic candidate, Grover Cleveland, who was trying to recapture the White House after losing it to Republican Benjamin Harrison four years before. Martha Truman did not share her husband's devout interest in politics (few women did at that time because they did not have the right to vote), and she felt little desire to accompany John to every political speech and rally held in town. But eight-year-old Harry did, enjoying each moment of the grand orations, the smoke-filled rooms, the loud talk and cheering. He was thrilled at wearing a campaign hat whose visor read GROVER CLEVELAND FOR PRESIDENT, but was openly disgusted at not being able to vote on election day.

It was almost a full extra day before the final election returns reached Independence. But when the news of Cleveland's victory finally arrived, it offered an opportunity for a grand parade through the town by his supporters. John Truman rode the finest gray mare he could find and helped to carry a wide banner proclaiming Cleveland's triumph. "We won!" young Harry shouted as his father passed by. It was a moment the boy would never forget. Yet he could little guess that an exciting adventure was only just beginning.

Chapter 2

Captain Harry of Battery D

"**N**o, no. That's not right, Charlie. Look at this picture of Caesar's bridge. If we're going to build a miniature replica of this bridge, we have to get everything in exact proportion to the original."

Charlie Ross pushed back his chair from the table, almost knocking over the carefully constructed framework of shaved sticks and tied boards. "Harry, we have to get this project in by tomorrow and I don't give a dead skunk's tail if it's inch by inch perfect or not."

"Well, I do!" Harry declared firmly. "I want us to win for the best Latin class project, and to do it we're going to have to work on this thing until we get it just right."

HIGH SCHOOL DAYS

Charlie Ross knew better than to argue with his best friend. When Harry Truman set out to do something in school, he did it right. If it caused his friends to become irritated, that was just too bad. Harry set high standards for himself, and he would not allow his weak eyesight and rather frail physical condition prevent him from reaching for high goals. He became respected for his determination and although not the most popular boy in his class, Harry was liked by his peers and appreciated by his teachers.

A new world of friends opened up to Harry when his father moved the family from Chrysler Street to Waldo Street in 1896. He earned a place in the Waldo Street Gang and spent his free time swimming, fishing, and camping. When the Spanish-American War began in 1898, the high school crowd on Waldo Street became more serious and organized a junior militia group. They gathered for weekly shooting drills with .22 caliber rifles and stood ready to help the American cause if needed. But the nation's military services proved equal to the problem without having to enlist the assistance of the Independence Junior Militia, so Harry and his friends continued their efforts in the classroom.

During his junior year in high school, Harry took a job as a clerk at Clinton's Drugstore, on the northeast corner of the town square. Although he hoped to go to college and knew he would have to contribute much of the money himself, he still would not allow his outside job to hinder his schoolwork or activities.

In his final year at Independence High, Harry helped to initiate a school newspaper called *The Gleam*. It gave him an opportunity to express his ideas on international, national, and school events as well as gather facts for news stories. This experience made him think about a future in journalism. "One who can use words well can communicate ideas and arouse emotions," Harry once wrote in *The Gleam*. "Certainly, one must appreciate the great responsibility in accepting such a task."

In 1901, at the age of 17, Harry graduated from Independence High School. He was not the class valedictorian—that honor went to his best friend, Charlie Ross—but there was little doubt that Harry was destined to tackle new challenges. For a brief time he entertained hopes of attending the United States Military Academy at West Point or the Naval Academy at Annapolis, but his poor eyesight

Harry Truman at 15 years of age, when he was a student at Independence High School. He achieved a reputation as a hard-working scholar and started the school newspaper. He graduated in 1901. (Harry S. Truman Library.)

squelched those plans. He then decided to work for a time and save his money; his father was experiencing financial problems and there were no extra funds for college.

MAKING MONEY

Finding a full-time job proved easier than Harry thought it might be for a new high school graduate. He was hired as a timekeeper for L. C. Smith, a railroad contractor. Always good with figures, Harry had no problem recording the hours spent working by the 400 men employed to lay new track. But his courage and patience were severely tested in getting along with the men who worked for Smith. Unaccustomed to their use of profane language and their heavy drinking habits, Harry was glad when a position became available as a bank clerk in nearby Kansas City. The new job paid five dollars more a month and posed no danger of being beaten up by a drunken worker. And since the bank was closed on weekends, Harry was able to find additional work as an usher at local theaters. It was a welcome escape from the "cage" he and the other clerks worked in at the bank.

It was while working at the bank that Kansas City welcomed President Theodore Roosevelt in 1904 as he swung through the Midwest on a speaking tour. With thousands of others, Harry stood and listened as the fiesty and fiery Roosevelt captivated his audience with stirring oratory and a beaming, wide smile. As the bank clerk turned and looked at the people around him, he was suddenly caught up in the magic of the moment — the excitement and thrill of imagining being so important as to command so much attention. Returning to look at the President of the United States, Truman felt a new awe and respect for Roosevelt, or rather any person who would serve in that position of leadership. It was a feeling that would last for the rest of his life.

John Truman continued to suffer financial setbacks. Vivian had joined Harry working in Kansas City but when their father asked his two sons to come back to help on the Grandview family farm, both boys agreed. Harry visited the U.S. Department of Agriculture's local Farm Bureau offices, updated himself on the latest innovations in agricultural technology, and applied what he learned. Within only a few years, production on the Truman farm had increased 50 percent.

But Harry was not all work and no play. With cousins scattered throughout the area, he found himself attending countless parties and picnics at the invitation of his relatives. His attention focused on an Independence girl, Bess Wallace, who he had met in Sunday School when the family first arrived in the city. She had been a member of the Waldo Street Gang, yet the shy Truman had not taken a serious interest in her until high school. Now, however, there was little doubt that Bess Wallace meant something special to the young Grandview farmer.

It was during this time that Harry Truman first came to understand a few fundamentals of politics. Although hardly considered a major business success, John Truman was liked and respected by people throughout the area. Men and women alike listened to him when he discussed politics, and he was considered an influential representative of the Democratic Party. Two local brothers, Tom and Mike Pendergast, recognized the positive role John Truman had among his peers. They used their political power to have him appointed an elections judge in Grandview. It took little convincing to get Harry to agree to be his father's clerk, as he had always appreciated the excitement of politics.

With Harry seated behind the wheel of his 1911 Stafford, friends (left to right) Natalie Wallace, Mrs. William Southern, Frank Gates Wallace, and Bess Wallace head for a favorite picnic site near the Little Blue River in 1915. (Harry S. Truman Library.)

STORM CLOUDS

Working a prospering farm, dating the girl he wished, helping in local politics – all was going well for Harry S. Truman until 1914. In that year, an assassin's bullet struck down Austria's Archduke Francis Ferdinand, a murder triggering the spark that would begin World War I. Then, as if a tragic echo of the archduke's death, John Truman died following surgery for an intestinal block.

As the older son, Harry had to assume new responsibilities for his family and the farm. Out of their respect for his father and in recognition of his added duties, the Pendergasts offered Harry the job of Grandview postmaster, which paid 50 dollars a month. But because he did not know anything about the position and was busy with the farm, Harry passed the postmaster spot along to a family friend who wanted the job and badly needed the money. Instead, hoping to realize healthy financial returns, Harry invested funds first in a lead and zinc mine in Oklahoma, then in an oil scheme. But when both investments failed, he decided to concentrate on the farm's proven assets.

When the United States entered World War I in April 1917, Harry Truman could have asked to be excused from military service because he was a working farmer. However, such a thought would never have occurred to him, particularly since he had served briefly in the National Guard while working in Kansas City. After he decided to enter the service, Truman contacted the members of his old National Guard outfit, Battery B Company. Secretly, he hoped the men might elect him a section sergeant (at that time, enlisted National Guardsmen chose their own officers through voting), but Harry got more than he hoped. The men of the Second Missouri Field Artillery elected him a first lieutenant.

They were all sworn into the United States Army in

A member of the Missouri National Guard while farming in Grandview, Harry wore his Battery B uniform with pride. (Harry S. Truman Library.)

August of 1917, officially becoming the 129th Artillery of the 35th Division. Assigned to Battery F, Harry was sent to Fort Sill, Oklahoma, where he helped run a soldiers' canteen. His skill with numbers helped the canteen make money, an unusual feat for a canteen.

INTO BATTLE WITH THE "DIZZY D" BATTERY

Early in 1918 Truman received orders to head overseas to France. Before he left, he made certain everything was taken care of with his family on the farm. Bess promised to wait for him and gave him a picture that he promised to carry with him "everywhere I go."

Landing in France on April 13, 1918, First Lieutenant Truman was assigned to Camp Coetquidan for instruction in French artillery. A quick and able student, he was soon promoted to captain and put in charge of Battery D. It was a dubious honor at best because the 188 men in the battery were known for their wild and rough behavior. Nicknamed "Dizzy D" by other officers and soldiers, this collection of loudmouths and ruffians had already gone through three commanding officers before Captain Truman arrived, and they had no intention of sparing him. But Harry refused to be influenced by their past record. After inspecting his troops for the first time, the new commander told his noncommissioned officers, "I didn't come here to get along with you guys. You're going to have to get along with me. If any of you think you can't, speak right up and I'll give you a punch in the nose." There was no reply.

A Trick Backfires

Captain Truman talked tough and acted tough, but the men of Battery D decided to find out how tough he really was.

*This rare picture of Harry S. Truman without his glasses was
used on his identification card for the American Expeditionary
Forces during World War I. (Harry S. Truman Library.)*

Late one night several of them turned loose all the horses
in the stockade. Since the horses were used to pulling big
guns and not having the freedom to run, the quiet of the
darkness was broken by the sounds of 160 stampeding animals.
"We'll all be killed!" someone shouted, with the rest of the
men closely watching the captain's tent. As expected, Truman
emerged, but he was not confused and frightened as the
soldiers had anticipated. After a lifetime of being around
horses, the captain knew these were not runaways. He simply
turned to those he suspected of being the ringleaders and
ordered the horses rounded up, wiped down, and put to bed.
Then he went back into his tent, leaving the men of Battery
D feeling more than a bit foolish.

Sneak Attack

One night Captain Truman and his men camped near an orchard. German soldiers were in the vicinity but orders had been given not to fire on them unless they attacked first. Unable to sleep, Truman spotted a German outfit preparing to launch a surprise attack. Before he could warn his troops, the Germans started bombarding the American forces. Still new to active combat, first one of the members of Battery D panicked, then another. Within minutes the entire group was in turmoil. They scrambled to the rear as fast as they could, leaving their guns and equipment.

At first Truman tried to rally his men with a few shouts. "No, men, stay!" he ordered. "Don't run like animals!" No one listened. Shells exploded on every side, sending giant tremors across the land and huge clouds of smoke into the air. Furious, red-faced Truman positioned himself midst the exploding shells. Every curse and cussword he had ever heard thundered out of him. "It turned the air blue," noted the regimental chaplain. But the sight of the short, bespectacled captain wildly waving his arms and shouting every filthy insult he could, stopped many of the retreating soldiers. Many of the men were Irish and took particular pride in their honor and courage. Here stood their leader, challenging—no, *attacking*—their heritage. Was he so brave? Who was he to be calling them names? Well, if this foulmouthed little gutter snake could face the Germans, so could they. Quickly the men returned to their positions. When finally ordered to retreat for their own safety, the men did so in an orderly fashion.

That skirmish became known to the men of Battery D as "The Battle of Who Run." After it was over, Captain Harry S. Truman was looked on with admiration and respect. His men knew he was strict but fair.

During the final months of the war, as the Germans retreated, "Captain Harry" led his Battery D troops through

Captain Harry S. Truman, Battery D, 129th Field Artillery, inspects Camp Coetquidan in Brittany, France, in July of 1918. (Harry S. Truman Library.)

muddy streets and roads, being shot at by sharpshooters left behind. Finally, on November 11, 1918, news came of a cease fire. World War I was over.

Many American officers proudly gave out medals to the men who had distinguished themselves in battle. Truman's immediate commander had little use for such rewards. This did not bother Captain Harry. "I did what had to be done," he declared modestly. "I didn't do anything out of the ordinary. I was not wounded and I got no citations of any kind."

The men of Battery D knew better. When they returned to New York City in April of 1919, Truman's men chipped in and bought him a silver loving cup. "To Captain Harry from Battery D" read the engraving. It was worth far more than any medal to the farmer from Grandview, Missouri.

Chapter 3
Pennies, Pains, and Politics

June 28, 1919. The Trinity Episcopal Church in Independence was filled to overflowing as townspeople gathered for the wedding of Harry S. Truman and Bess Elizabeth Wallace. Many members of Battery D were there in cleanly pressed military uniforms. The ceremony itself was short and simple. "There was no need for a long ceremony," the new groom remarked later at the reception in the Wallace home. "After all, the courtship lasted 29 years. I think I was in love with her when I was six years old and had just come to town." Bess smiled. "My husband is a deliberate man," she offered.

Deliberate as Truman may have been in courtship, he wasted no time in finding a new business enterprise. Tired of farming, he contacted an old army buddy named Eddie Jacobson, whom he'd worked with at the soldiers' canteen in Fort Sill. Together, they had turned the military operation into a moneymaker—why, then, couldn't they share their business sense in civilian life? All the men coming home from the war would need shirts, suits, ties, gloves, and hats. In November of 1919, Truman and Jacobson's Men's Clothing Store opened for business.

Truman worked long hours at the store. He opened its doors every morning at eight o'clock. After clerking all day, Harry closed up at nine at night and checked the day's sales. Jacobson clerked at the store, too, and also served as the buyer. The two men kept their store open six days a week,

Harry and his new wife, Bess, share a quiet moment on the afternoon of their wedding, June 28, 1919. (Harry S. Truman Library.)

often welcoming many of their past army buddies who not only spent a few dollars but relived war days in conversation. The times immediately following the war were good and the haberdashery thrived.

But in 1921, falling farm prices caused a snowballing effect that closed many businesses and put people out of work. Truman and Jacobson cut their prices, but fewer and fewer customers came into their store. With creditors demanding payment, the haberdashery store closed its doors for the last time in 1922. Jacobson suggested declaring bankruptcy, but Harry would not even hear of such an idea. "If it takes years to do, I'll pay off every penny we owe," Truman promised, and he did exactly that. It took him 15 years.

BECOMING A CANDIDATE

Despite his disappointment over the failed business, Truman was not one to dwell on the past. His decision to make a try in the political arena surprised few people because he was always known to be well-informed and full of opinions of how government might be improved. Frequently, he shared the stories of his own childhood—of the political rallies he attended with his father, of the speeches belted out by candidates, of cheering crowds and thunderous applause. Yes, it was all a vivid part of his memory, and it seemed only natural that he should run for election himself.

Truman knew his choices for elected office were limited because he had no law degree or college diploma. Yet the position of county judge or commissioner was open to anyone who wanted to run. Despite the label of "judge," no courtrooms were involved. The county judge helped set and collect taxes, assisted with the management of homes for delinquent children and the elderly, and supervised the repair of county roads and government buildings.

Proprietor Harry Truman with customers in his Kansas City haberdashery. The men's clothing store would enjoy only a three-year lifespan, from 1919 until 1922. (Harry S. Truman Library.)

Truman knew he could never win an election without help. Two families, the Pendergasts and the Shannons, controlled the political machinery of the Democratic Party in Jackson County, Missouri. Harry knew the Pendergasts from earlier dealings with his father. And for a time, Mike Pendergast's son Jim and Harry were both lieutenants with the 129th Artillery during the war. Truman didn't know anyone in the Shannon family, so he decided to call on the Pendergasts. Jim was delighted to see his wartime buddy, listened to his plans for seeking election, then promised to pass the word along to his father and uncle.

Tom and Mike Pendergast knew that Harry Truman had many friends who would vote for him. But party machinery was not all that simple. "You'll have to win the Democratic nomination on your own," Mike Pendergast told the eager Truman. "If you can get the nomination on your own, we'll throw all our support behind you in the election."

Fair enough, Truman thought. Carefully, he made plans to run for county judge. First of all, he had to have a car. Seven townships made up the Jackson County district. It was important to attend every political gathering that was scheduled, whether it was a small picnic or big town parade. Truman knew that many people did not care to attend open public events but preferred to talk with candidates at their own homes. Because that was Truman's favorite way of meeting people, he mapped out the entire area in a way that would give him a chance for many house-to-house stops.

Truman bought an old Dodge roadster and started campaigning. Once he reached the rural roads in Jackson County, potholes loomed large and ominous, almost daring the would-be judge to plunge into them. Although he could not afford it, Truman had no choice but to invest his last few dollars in some bags of cement that weighed the Dodge down and kept it from bouncing him out.

Mudslinging began early in the campaign with a full blast of criticisms and accusations directed at Truman. His opponents ridiculed him for his lack of business sense, based on the failure of the clothing store. When one of his challengers managed to get hold of past voting records, he discovered that Harry had voted for a Republican in 1920, and publicly denounced Truman's right to be the Democratic candidate. "Sure, I voted for John Miles when he ran for county marshal," Truman fired back, "and I'd do it again, too. I was closer to John Miles than a brother. In the war, I have seen him hold the American line when only John Miles and his three batteries were between the Germans and a successful counterattack. He was of the right stuff, and a man who wouldn't vote for his comrade under circumstances such as these would be untrue to his country. I have no apology to make."

Facing the Klan

Across the country, and in Jackson County as well, the Ku Klux Klan was flexing its muscle. Claiming its goal was to strengthen the nation, the organization spread its own campaign of religious and racial hatred. Many of Truman's buddies in the war joined the Klan. "You should, too, Captain, if you want to win the primary." Truman was suspicious of the group, yet he agreed to join. After all, he did not have to attend their meetings or support their causes; he simply would add his name to the membership list.

It was not that easy. When Truman showed up to be admitted, Klan leaders demanded that the candidate make promises if elected. "You can't give a Catholic a job if you belong to our group," they told him. Truman could not believe his ears. His face reddened in anger, the veins of his temples bulged. "I'll give whoever I want a job if I'm elected," he exclaimed, "and no jackass in white robes and hood will stop me!" Truman was ordered from the room, but he had already slammed the door.

It was a long and bitter campaign. Even after the votes were cast, rumors spread that the ballot boxes would be stolen. But the county marshal made sure that did not happen, and Truman won the election by 500 votes.

Compared to winning the Democratic nomination, the campaign against the Republican candidate in the November election was easy. Truman took the oath of office as county judge in January of 1923.

Once Harry had familiarized himself with all of his duties, it was difficult to know where to begin. Because of shabby workmanship, even recently repaired county roads needed to be fixed. And because of poor management, many of the county institutions had to be taken over by the state for proper maintenance and supervision. Unpaid bills were found in desk drawers, while creditors demanded payment for supplies and services. "I thought we had debts with the haberdashery," the new judge told his wife, "but you would never believe the mess this county is in!"

There was little to be gained by complaining, however, and Truman began working with another county judge, Henry McElroy, to whittle away the financial deficits. In visits to Chicago and St. Louis, Harry was successful in obtaining low-interest loans for the county, applying the borrowed funds toward paying off major debts. By the time Truman's first term as county judge ended in 1924, over $600,000 of the county's past bills had been paid off, and many of the roads had been repaired.

Truman Becomes a Father

On February 17, 1924, Bess and Harry Truman became proud parents of a baby girl born in the family home on North Delaware Street in Independence. The baby was christened

Harry's "Boss"

Harry met Bess Wallace shortly after the Truman family moved to Independence, Missouri, in December of 1890. For the next 80 years, the two of them enjoyed a relationship that grew from friendship into love. Married on June 28, 1919, the devoted couple enjoyed over 53 years of marriage before Harry's death on December 26, 1972.

Growing up in Independence, Bess Wallace was a popular young girl, always surrounded by friends. She enjoyed fishing, playing cards, and going dancing. Sports were a major love, and she excelled at basketball, tennis, and baseball.

Harry's major interests stemmed from books. He loved to talk about the deeds of great people, their roles in building countries and making history. He took piano lessons and could play for hours.

Despite their different interests, Bess and Harry fell in love. They shared the fun of going on picnics and to concerts. They laughed together at vaudeville performances, imitating the performers. Always they poked fun at each other. Whenever one of them became "uppity" about anything, the other could quickly find a joke to lighten the situation.

Bess' mother, Madge Gates Wallace, seldom encouraged the relationship. She regarded her daughter as bright and poised, a fine catch for the proper young man. As a common dirt farmer without a college education, Harry was hardly a top candidate.

But love won out. Clearly, Bess saw in Harry much more potential than her mother did. After all, surely a man's worth was measured by more than how much money he had in the bank or how much education he had acquired.

It soon became clear that Harry was happiest when serving the public. This meant "living in a fishbowl" for all to see. The bowl was a small tank in Missouri, but it became a giant aquarium after Harry went to Washington. It was a life Bess reluctantly accepted. With grace and charm, she carried out the duties of a Washington hostess. Undoubtedly, as White House servants prepared and served their meals, there were countless times when Bess would have preferred making a meatloaf herself in her kitchen on Delaware Street in Independence.

Knowing how much Harry enjoyed having her along, Bess frequently accompanied him on campaign trips. He loved introducing her as "The Boss." Some of his opponents used the nickname against Harry, suggesting that Bess made his decisions and plans. It was hardly the case, although she *was* a trusted confidante.

Following Harry's death in 1972, Bess continued to live in the family home on Delaware Street. Her greatest joys were visits by her four grandchildren and pride in her daughter Margaret's writing success. An accomplished biographer, whose works about her parents provide rare insight into their

> fascinating family life, Margaret has also
> achieved recognition as a master mystery
> author. Many of her books reflect her knowl-
> edge of Washington, D.C.
>   Bess Truman died on October 18, 1982,
> in Independence. She was 97 years old at the
> time of her death.

Mary Margaret. Noting that both parents were approaching 40, one reporter carelessly asked if that wasn't a bit late to be having children. "Didn't know there were set ages for such things," Truman snapped. "Maybe you know something we don't."

As busy as he was serving as a county judge and being a new father, Truman also attended classes at the Kansas City Law School. He was convinced that a public official should have a law degree.

Riding a Rollercoaster

Satisfied that he had done the best job he could, Harry faced re-election as county judge with confidence. But the campaign quickly turned ugly. The Ku Klux Klan had gained members and power in Jackson County. They had not forgotten Truman's rejection of them. They attacked him at every opportunity, their leader writing in the Kansas City newspaper, "We are unalterably opposed to Harry Truman." Urged by Democratic leaders to patch up the open wounds with the KKK, Truman refused. "They're a bunch of un-American, cheap fakers who are afraid to come out from behind their own bedsheets!" he declared, adding fuel to the campaign fire.

The usually smooth-running Democratic machinery in

Jackson County badly needed oiling. Leaders within the party fought among themselves. Little attention was given the candidates. Truman received more help from some Republicans, including the editor of the *Kansas City Star.* Praising Judges McElroy and Truman, the editorial stated, "Tuesday the Democratic voters of Jackson County will show whether they are interested enough in good service to renominate the men who were responsible for the remarkable showing made." The editorial commended the two men for reducing the county debt and rebuilding bad roads.

Despite the favorable editorial, when the voters in Jackson County went to the polls in November of 1924, it was clear that the attacks by the Ku Klux Klan and the internal squabbling within the Democratic Party had done severe damage to Truman's candidacy. He lost the election by 867 votes. Once again, Harry S. Truman was a man without work, and this time he had both a wife and a child to support. These were dark days for the man from Missouri, and the future looked grim.

Chapter 4
Off to Washington

Accepting his defeat at the polls as only a temporary setback, Truman quickly looked around for employment. By this time, he was determined to someday become a presiding judge for Jackson County, then a United States representative, governor, and finally, a United States senator. But for the moment, there was need to pay the daily bills, so Harry took a job selling memberships in the Kansas City Automobile Club. Friends and political associates were eager and willing to help, enabling him to sell over 1,000 memberships in one year. It was worth double the income he had made serving as a judge.

When two friends approached him with the prospect of taking over the Security State Bank of Englewood, Truman agreed. The price was a "steal"—$30,000—and no down payment was required. Unfortunately, Truman soon discovered the price was not the only "steal" in the arrangement. A check of the bank's records revealed that the previous owner was guilty of misusing depositors' money. After taking the information to the bank's bonding company, Truman washed his hands of the entire enterprise.

BACK INTO POLITICS

In 1925, Truman became a partner in the Independence Community Savings and Loan Association, a venture that helped fill the family coffers a bit. Yet the work with banks and financing did nothing to satisfy Harry's appetite for politics. He yearned to again serve in some kind of governmental capacity, and by 1926 he was ready to run for election as the presiding judge of Jackson County. The Pendergast family was more than willing to throw the support of their party machinery behind him. This time there was no long line of Democratic opponents opposing his right to carry the party banner into battle against the Republicans. Truman campaigned with fresh fire and vigor, lambasting the entire opposition with quotes and quips that brought loud laughter and clapping. "Why, those Republicans wouldn't know a pothole in the road if they fell in one and were never heard from again!" Truman bellowed. "If you want something done right, elect a Democrat, and I just happen to be Harry S. Truman and I want you to remember that name on election day!"

The voters of Jackson County did exactly that, thrusting Truman into the seat of presiding judge by a margin of 16,000 votes. He felt it was a mandate, a major vote of confidence by the people allowing him the right to streamline any area of government inefficiency.

Once again, he found that construction of county roads had fallen desperately behind. Worse yet, that which had been done, had been done poorly. Engineers he sent out to inspect recently constructed roads labeled them "piecrusts" that would need immediate replacement and repair. Under Truman's direction, a whole new system of county roads was proposed at a cost of seven million dollars.

Knowing that such an amount could not be raised without help, Truman went to Tom Pendergast for his support. The Democratic chieftain sadly shook his head, declaring, "You'll never get people to vote that kind of money for roads." Such a declaration merely made Truman even more determined to get the job done. He visited every county group and organization that would listen. He offered to award contracts based on low bids and promised to establish a bipartisan board of engineers to oversee the project.

Tom Pendergast continued to shake his head when Truman sought Republican support for the new road system. Surprisingly, however, the Republicans threw their backing behind the Democratic judge and his program. On May 8, 1928, Truman's 44th birthday, the voters of Jackson County passed a bond issue for financing new roads by a three-fourths majority.

A COUNTRY IN CHAOS

As the 1920s drew to a close, the American business world was dealt a staggering blow. On October 24, 1929, the stock market "crashed," creating turmoil in the financial and commercial flow of money that maintains the nation's economy. Businesses failed, banks closed, and millions of people lost their jobs.

Leaders of the National Democratic Party rallied behind Franklin Delano Roosevelt as their presidential candidate to turn around the country's economy. After his election in 1932, Roosevelt innovated one program after another aimed at getting the country back on its feet. And Judge Harry Truman did the same in Jackson County, Missouri. He led the fight for a bond issue that would finance the building of a new city hall in Kansas City, a new county office structure, more playgrounds, a modern county hospital, a new police facility, and a new waterworks. "We'll be not only giving ourselves the quality of life that we need in this area, but we will be putting our unemployed back to work. People need to be active, to be contributing." Truman's words struck a responsive chord in the hearts and heads of those in Jackson County. Because they sounded like an echo of those spoken by President Franklin Roosevelt, few were surprised when Truman's name became mentioned more and more often as a possible candidate for higher office.

Certainly Truman did little to discourage such talk. Politics offered a challenge and excitement he had never known before. It was the business of people and power—a feeling of getting things done and making things better. Exhilarating—yes, that's what it was. A feeling of being useful, creative, worthwhile. Nothing was quite like it.

The Dark Side of Politics

Not that being a public figure was all cheerful and bright. There was a dark side, too. Politics could be an ugly game, with name-calling and insults tossed around recklessly; with underhanded gossip and rumor staining reputation and family. That was another thing—family. Politics, being known to the public, brought special problems to the entire family.

One afternoon Truman received a disturbing telephone call from Bess. Someone had gone to Margaret's school and told the first grader's teacher that he was supposed to take "Mary Margaret, Judge Truman's little girl, home." Though christened Mary Margaret, the youngster went by the name Margaret in school. Not recognizing the stranger, the school called Bess. Bess, in turn, called Truman. "Don't worry. I'll handle it," Truman comforted his wife. Not wasting a moment, he sent police hurrying to the school, where they found that the mysterious stranger had disappeared. From that day on, Truman made sure Margaret never went to or from school alone.

Yes, politics had its negative side, there was no doubt about that. But there were so many rewards, so many intangible satisfactions. Certainly the new buildings constructed and services provided while he served as a Jackson County judge offered Truman a feeling of accomplishment. But there was another feeling inside Truman—a feeling to move on to even greater challenges.

The Pendergasts' political machinery was still in control of Jackson County despite Mike Pendergast's death in 1929. Truman knew that Tom Pendergast did not appreciate his unwillingness to hire the people he sent over to the office of the county judge. "You've got to play ball with us if you want our help," Tom insisted. "I'll only play ball if you pitch straight," Harry fired back. "Send me a qualified man and I'll hire him. Just don't send me dummies with sawdust in their heads."

INTO THE SENATE

Despite Tom Pendergast's misgivings about Truman, the political baron had little choice but to turn to the popular county judge as a candidate for the United States Senate. Three other possible candidates refused to accept the help of the Pendergast political machinery, but Truman was more than willing. "You know how I operate," he told the political boss. "You know a darnsight more than I do about this business. But I'll be the same man whether I'm a senator or not. I'll always be willing to listen, but don't expect me to take orders. I make up my own mind." Reluctantly, Pendergast agreed to help. Harry S. Truman became a candidate for United States senator from the state of Missouri.

Truman was the underdog in the Democratic primary. The *Kansas City Star* noted, "It is agreed Pendergast has taken on a real job. To jump a man from the county court bench to a Senate nomination is quite an undertaking." Privately, Pendergast did not give Truman a chance. Two popular U.S. congressmen wanted the Democratic nomination, too. Jacob "Tuck" Milligan was backed by the other present Missouri senator, Bennett Clark. Congressman John Cochran of St.

Louis also wanted his chance at the Senate seat. It was a rough three-man race. Observers called it "a three-ring circus."

Quickly Truman's opponents labeled him "Pendergast's boy," suggesting that to back him one joined gangsters and thugs of the lowest nature. Truman reminded the voters that both Milligan and Cochran had begged for Pendergast's support when they sought election as congressmen. "It's a lot different now," Truman noted, "when my rivals want to distance themselves from a former supporter. Well, I'm guilty of standing by my friends."

While the mudslinging continued, Truman lifted the campaign to a higher level. He emphasized his personal desire to work side-by-side with President Franklin Roosevelt. "The President's New Deal concept is putting this country back on its feet. It is providing jobs to those who will work and offering programs to those who need help most. That's exactly what Harry S. Truman has been trying to do, and I'll hope you let both of us get on with our duties."

During a hot July, the county judge traveled the state, giving 15–16 speeches every day. "Slow down," some advisors told Truman. "You can't talk to every voter in the state." Truman shook his head. "I can sure as tarnation try, can't I?"

The primary was held August 7, 1934. Although Truman had waged a vigorous campaign that far outdistanced his opponents in miles covered and speeches given, pollsters predicted that Truman would lose. Early election returns backed up that feeling, with Cochran leading by almost 100,000 votes at midnight. "It doesn't look good," Harry told Bess. "Might as well go to bed." But as vote counts continued to come in, Cochran's lead began to dwindle. The people in farms and the little towns, the folks Truman had personally gone out to meet, turned the tables on his opponents. When the final vote was counted, Truman had won by almost 40,000 votes.

While sadly noting Tom Pendergast's hold on Missouri's Democratic Party, the *Kansas City Star* nevertheless heaped praise on the party's presiding judge. "Jackson County has found him a capable and honest public official, a man of unimpeachable character and integrity." Truman found this editorial, contained in the pages of a well-known Republican newspaper, a useful item of campaign ammunition as he opened his race for the Senate seat. But he noted with a sense of hurt that his old high school friend, Charlie Ross, mourned his selection in the editorial pages of the *St. Louis Post Dispatch:* "Under our political system, an obscure man can be made the nominee of a major political party for the high office of United States Senator by virtue of the support given him by a city boss." The newspaper had been an open backer of John Cochran. But Truman, whose loyalty to old friends was a major part of his character, felt deeply wounded.

Victory Trail

There was little time for personal grief, however. The November election was just around the corner. Getting his second wind, Truman opened his campaign against the incumbent Republican senator, Roscoe Patterson. Once more, Truman tied his own ideas to those of Franklin Roosevelt. It was easy to take the pulse of America, easier still to judge the Missouri climate politically. The nation was getting back on its feet under President Roosevelt. Why disrupt the process? "Our President needs help to continue rebuilding the country," Truman asserted as he criss-crossed the state. "Let's send people who will help him in the Senate, not Republicans who will undermine his every effort." Clearly, the Missouri voters, and voters in states across the country, were listening. Candidates supporting Roosevelt won elections everywhere. Truman did not waste a minute. Always a quick reader, he boned up on the backgrounds of the other men in the Senate, carefully analyzing their opinions and styles. Hour after hour, he poured over books, magazine articles, and newspaper clippings, mentally digesting each new piece of information he came upon. "If I am going to be an effective senator," Harry told Bess, "I've got to know how to work with these fellas."

A Different World

Shortly after his arrival in the Senate during January of 1935, one of the leaders helped to put Truman at ease. "The first six months you're here, you'll wonder how you got here," observed Senator Hamilton Lewis of Illinois. "After that, you'll wonder how the rest of us got here." But the light-hearted exchanges were few for Truman in those early days in the Senate chambers. The majority of senators kept their distance from the so-called "Pendergast puppet from Missouri." There were days when Truman wanted to grab the podium and shout, "I'm my own man and no one has ever made me do anything against my principles!" But it was a fleeting thought, a useless idea, and Truman simply gritted his teeth and stood the pain that comes from feeling rejected. He had learned such lessons in childhood.

Perhaps what troubled Truman even more was the effect that moving to Washington had on Bess and Margaret. They had to give up a 14-room house for a four-room apartment, not to mention leaving behind family and friends. There were bills from the campaign that had to be paid, and even a few payments left from the old haberdashery business. It seemed ironic that a man who had once been a partner in a men's clothing business had to rent a morning suit so he could be sworn in as a senator.

Shortly after moving into the Washington apartment, Truman made the rounds of the capital's music stores. In each one, he sat down at every available piano and played. Finally he found one he wanted, paid the five dollars a month rent, and scheduled its delivery. The moment the piano arrived, 10-year-old Margaret ran to it and began playing. She had inherited her father's love for music and having a piano in the apartment was like welcoming a friend from home. Truman slid on the bench beside his daughter and shared the keyboard. It was a rare moment, for in the months to follow he would have little time to play. But the sound of his daughter's playing was a perfect accompaniment to the endless pages of documents he studied in preparation for his work in the Senate.

Chapter 5
Out of the Shadows

One morning Truman and his secretary sat at a big table. Carefully they studied the application folders before them. One of the pleasures of being a United States senator was being able to single out young men for appointments to the Military Academy at West Point. Truman looked at folder after folder, 50 of them in all, most bulging with impressive letters of recommendation from well-known politicians and educators back in Missouri. Finally, Truman opened a folder that contained only a single letter from the applicant, written in pencil but displaying candid honesty and desire.

"Let's give the appointment to this young man," Truman said. His secretary wore a surprised look. "Yes, I know it doesn't look like much on the surface. But I think I can judge character and I like what this boy says and how he says it. Anybody can buy fancy stationery."

READING AND ROUTINE

There were days when Truman felt like the young boy with the pencil. Still self-conscious about not having a college education or a law degree, Truman often glanced around the Senate in awe of his colleagues. He knew many of them were looking at him, too. Tom Pendergast was being investigated for corruption within his political machine. Although Truman was innocent of any crime or misservice, there was always a feeling of guilt by association. It was difficult to work under such a dark cloud of doubt and suspicion.

But work Truman did. Rising at 5:30 each morning, he first read the newspapers, then he ate breakfast and went for a brisk walk. By eight o'clock he was in his office. There was always mail to answer and visitors from Missouri who wanted to talk with their senator. Committee meetings usually started at 10, and at noon he went to the Senate for business there.

All afternoon and often into the evening, discussion and debate occupied his attention. Before heading home, he went to the office to take care of any last-minute items of the day. Arriving back at the family apartment, Harry enjoyed visiting with Bess and Margaret over dinner. He willingly accepted the task of drying the dishes. Before going to bed, he often spent a few hours reading the bills that had come before the Senate that day.

A Senate "Plodder"

Presiding over the Senate was Vice-President of the United States John Nance Garner. A Texan, Garner took an immediate liking to Truman. "We folks from the Southwest speak with the same twang," Garner laughed. "Just relax, boy. Every fellow in this chamber has his own way of doin' things, his own style. Some of 'em should have been on the stage as performers. You strike me as bein' more of a plodder. It's the plodders that get the real work done around here."

Garner had sized up Truman perfectly. Efficient and organized, he had no desire to make newspaper headlines. It took him four months before he had written a bill he considered worthy of his colleagues' attention. It was another two months before he rose to speak in the Senate chamber. No, Truman much preferred the order and quiet of committee hearings.

Appointed to the Senate Appropriations Committee, Harry became an expert on military and defense spending. Patiently and politely he questioned the army and navy officers who appeared before the committee. They were impressed with how well prepared Truman always seemed to be. He expressed concern that the American army was not as well prepared as it should be. Troubled by the build-up of Germany's military forces, under the leadership of Adolph Hitler, Harry suggested additional spending for the armed services in this country. But few people listened. After all, the United States was at peace. There were plenty of other places where money could be spent.

Reforming the Railroads

Truman was also a member of the Interstate Commerce Committee. Senator Burton Wheeler of Montana served as chairman of this group. When Wheeler formed a subcommittee to investigate the railroads late in 1936, he did not choose Truman as a member. Nonetheless, Harry sat in on the subcommittee meetings. Poor conditions of the railroads had long been a problem in Missouri, and he hoped to find out why. When a spot opened up on the subcommittee, Wheeler invited Truman to serve and he accepted without hesitation. When other duties took Wheeler and several subcommittee members away, Harry was named vice-chairman to keep proceedings moving.

The choice was a wise one. Truman quickly assigned staff aides to go out and investigate how each railroad line was operated. "We've got to find out why we've got so many problems with this industry," he insisted. "Customers who ride trains are sometimes risking their lives with some of the machinery being used. Common stockholders are cheated out of dividends that are due them. Too many fat cats are getting rich at the expense of Mr. Average American."

Owners of the railroads and their lobbyists pressured Truman to stop his investigations. Letters poured into his office by the thousands, supposedly coming from concerned citizens. As he read a few letters, Truman felt his anger rise. Each message was the same, almost word for word. "Those confounded lobbyists have gone out and lied to Americans across the country!" he exclaimed. He read a few more of the letters. They were all the same. "Burn 'em! Burn 'em all. We'll get to the truth all right. If there's anything that makes my blood boil, it's folks who will go out and lie deliberately to make a few bucks."

Countless witnesses were called before the subcommittee. Truman did most of the questioning himself. He demanded to know exactly where profits were spent, how often repairs were made, what safety steps were taken on every railroad. "You expect too much," one railroad president carelessly told Truman. "Why should I know everything you're asking?" "Because you're responsible for the safe transportation of thousands of men, women, and children!" Truman snapped back. "And because you're getting paid plenty of money to know the answers!"

Truman was convinced that the railroad companies had become too big. They took no time to consider the best interests of the individuals who rode on their trains. The railroad executives simply wanted to make as much money as they could without spending what was needed to keep their facilities safe.

Feeling the same way and offering his support was Justice Louis D. Brandeis of the U.S. Supreme Court. A graduate of Harvard Law School, Brandeis had been appointed to the Court by President Woodrow Wilson in 1916. The distinguished judge took a special liking to Truman and spent many evenings having long talks with him. Truman listened closely to everything Judge Brandeis had to say. "Talking to this man is like taking law at night school," Harry told Bess. Other lawyers joined the evening sessions, and economists too. Truman was fascinated by the discussions about the Constitution, foreign treaties, domestic laws, and other issues.

Speaking Out

Reluctant to speak out against the railroad leaders for fear it might appear he merely wanted headlines, Truman finally reached a point where he could no longer remain silent. In a speech in June of 1937, he told his fellow senators, "Some of the country's greatest railroads have been deliberately looted by their financial agents." He then went on to recount two railroad holdups by the outlaw Jesse James, one of the Rock Island Lines and the other of the Missouri Pacific. The first holdup brought the notorious bandit $3,000; the second, $17,000. Thirty years later, Truman continued, "the Rock Island went through a looting by some gentlemen known as the 'Tin Plate Millionaires.' They used no guns, but they ruined the railroad and got away with $70 million or more . . ."

Six months later, Truman again rose to speak in the Senate. This time he took a stand against big business and the concentration of wealth in the hands of just a few. "One of the difficulties as I see it is that we worship money instead of honor." Truman paused, gazing around the Senate chamber. "A billionaire in our estimation is much greater in the eyes of the people than a public servant who works for the public interest."

Continuing, Truman pointed out the dangers of having so much money, so much power in the hands of only a few giant companies and their leaders. "I believe this country would be better off if we did not have 60 percent of the assets of all insurance companies concentrated in four companies. I believe that a thousand insurance companies with four million dollars each in assets would be just a thousand times better for the country than the Metropolitan Life with four billion dollars in assets . . . a thousand county seats of 7,000 each are a thousand times more important to this Republic than one city of seven million. Our unemployment and our unrest are the result of the concentration of wealth, the concentration of population in industrial centers, mass production, and a lot of other so-called modern improvements." Applause filled the Senate as Harry nodded and returned to his seat.

John Nance Garner had been right. Truman's "plodding" style, unflashy but thorough, won him more and more respect from both Democrats and Republicans in the Senate. Truman was sorry when Tom Pendergast and 258 of his political workers were sent to prison. At the same time, he was relieved when it was made public that there was not one shred of evidence that he had done anything improper while holding any office in Jackson County or in the Senate.

In January of 1939, Truman reported the complete findings of his investigation of the nation's railroads and spelled out recommendations for correcting the problems. Although action on Truman's suggestions came slowly, a bill making many reforms in the transportation industry was finally agreed on between the Senate and the House of Representatives. In 1940, President Roosevelt signed the Transportation Act. Truman was delighted, feeling his efforts had not been in vain.

"YOU JUST CAN'T WIN"

But the delight was short-lived. Truman's term in the Senate was due to expire in 1940. Without Pendergast to help, Harry wondered if he could win another term. He wanted to serve again; there was no question about that. The work was challenging and meaningful, co-workers had become friends, and Bess and Margaret seemed happy in Washington.

There were times, however, when Harry felt like he was the only one who wanted him to stay in the Senate. Governor Stark of Missouri announced that he also wanted the job. Worse than that, Truman received word that President Roosevelt wanted Stark too. Not that Harry would go unrewarded for his service—a position on the Interstate Commerce Commission was his for the asking. But Harry didn't want to serve on the Interstate Commerce Commission. He wanted to serve in the Senate again.

Hoping to drum up support, Truman invited 30 political and personal friends to meet with him in St. Louis. Only six of them appeared. Those who showed up told Truman that he did not have a chance. "You don't have any organized support." "You don't have money for a big campaign." "You haven't got any newspapers or companies behind you." "Even though nobody proved anything, some people still associate you with Boss Pendergast. Sorry, Harry. You just can't win." Truman listened to everything his friends said. The more they talked, the more determined he became to give it another try.

In February of 1940, Truman filed for re-election. As soon as he could, he started on an automobile campaign, reaching 75 counties in the state. Throughout the spring he spoke in every town and village that would hear him. Governor Stark, thinking President Roosevelt was going to pick him as a vice-presidential running mate, held off campaigning for the Senate seat. The delay gave Truman a good head start.

Needed—A Miracle or Two

Soon Truman's campaign funds dwindled. He could not afford any major radio or newspaper publicity. Up to a month before the August primary, it looked like only a miracle could help him. Then the closest thing to a miracle did happen. The railroad unions, remembering how hard Truman had fought against the greedy barons of their industry, endorsed the champion of their cause. They flooded the state with a special Truman edition of their newspaper. Another near-miracle occurred when St. Louis Mayor Bernard Dickmann, previously a Stark supporter, threw his support to Truman only two days before the primary.

The votes were cast on August 6. When early returns put Stark in the lead, Truman went to bed. He did not want to face the news of his defeat until morning. But there was no defeat to face. By the time all the votes were counted, Truman had carried the state by 8,000 votes. "I hope the news doesn't send Governor Stark raving mad!" the victorious incumbent quipped.

Senate Supporters

There was little doubt that whoever captured the Democratic primary in August would beat the Republican challenger in November. It still pleased Truman when many of his Senate colleagues offered to come to Missouri and speak on his behalf.

"Harry Truman is the hardest working senator in Washington," proclaimed his colleague, Senator Alben Barkley. "Just don't tell the folks back in Kentucky I said that. I've been telling them that *I* am!" And Senator Tom Connally of Texas noted that "if you want to know any fact or detail about any bill up for a vote in the chamber, you can ask Harry. He doesn't miss a thing."

Hoping to prevent a Democratic landslide, the Republican candidate, Manvel Davis, called Truman "a puppet that will dance for anyone pulling the strings, whether it be a Pendergast or a Roosevelt." Imitation ballots were circulated listing the Democratic candidate as Harry Solomon Truman. Accompanying the ballots, distributed by members of the Ku Klux Klan, were the whispers that Harry Truman had Jewish blood in his veins.

However, nothing could stop the Truman re-election bid. Staunchly defending President Roosevelt and his programs, Truman rolled over his opponent by more than 40,000 votes. When he flew back to Washington and entered the Senate chamber, every senator in the room rose to his feet and applauded. No longer would anyone think of Truman as a puppet. He had waged a strong fight to recapture his seat in the Senate, and he did it with honor. Truman smiled and waved. Yes, he liked this place. He liked it just fine!

Chapter 6

Harry Truman, Public Investigator

Silently, Truman closed the door. He glanced around the empty hallway. No one was in sight, but strange sounds came from around the corner. Harry tiptoed forward. As he rounded the corner, he discovered three men sleeping on the floor, snoring loudly.

"What in tarnation . . ."

Their sleep interrupted, the surprised trio jumped to their feet. They grabbed nearby tools and began hammering nails in planks of wood. Truman shook his head in disgust. He wrote a few notes on the clipboard he held and continued walking.

It was January 1941. Truman's earlier fears about the German leader Adolph Hitler had come true. Hitler's Nazi military machine was invading countries throughout Europe. No longer could America ignore the potential danger of the power-hungry dictator across the sea. "We must build an arsenal of democracy," declared President Roosevelt. "We must be on our guard." Twenty-five billion dollars worth of defense contracts went out to industries across the nation, active recruiting of soldiers and sailors began, and financial aid was sent to England to help fight off the German attackers.

GUARDIAN OF PUBLIC MONIES

But when Truman received letters that construction of the army base at Fort Leonard Wood in Rolla, Missouri, was riddled with waste, the senator decided to check out the situation personally. Not only did he find the place filled with sleeping workmen, he found tools and expensive machinery sitting unprotected under falling rain. Fences were wide open, doors unlocked, keys left in unmanned vehicles – no security system in operation. Figures revealed that the buildings were costing three and four times what they should.

Hoping that Fort Leonard Wood was just an isolated example, Truman headed to other Army camps and defense companies. He traveled 30,000 miles, carefully taking down facts and figures. He filled notebook after notebook. Everywhere he went, Harry found padded charges and waste. By the time he completed his inspections and reported his findings to his colleagues in the Senate, he could not control his anger. "We don't have to worry about any outside powers attacking us," Truman declared, his eyebrows raised and face red with disgust. "We're doing it to ourselves! We're tossing dollars into the wind and watching them fly away."

Having sounded the alarm, Truman urged the Senate to act. It did just that, appointing Truman chairman of a committee to investigate defense spending. Quickly the committee was dubbed "The Truman Committee." Only $15,000 was authorized for expenses. The senators thought Truman only intended to clean up the situation at Fort Leonard Wood, but he had other ideas.

Quickly, Truman organized a team of investigators. "I can't pay you what I would like," he told each member, "but I'm hoping you can see what your work could mean to your country." It was clear to everyone that this was an important job. Doubters had only to look at Truman's intense face and listen to his sincere voice. "Whether you're inspecting an aircraft factory, a mine, an explosives plant, a shipyard, everyone gets the same treatment. If they're doing what they're supposed to do, fine. But if they're wasting money or not living up to their government contracts, we'll go after them with every weapon we've got."

Staff members scattered across the country. They toured defense operations, checked their books, questioned officials. Unwilling to merely sit in Washington and review reports as they came in, Truman traveled too. Company leaders knew better than to try to influence Truman with fancy food and entertainment when he arrived at their operations. He was there for business only.

A Day of Infamy

It was while on such a mission that Truman received an early morning phone call from Washington. He was staying in a hotel in Columbia, Missouri. The minute he heard Bess' voice he knew something was wrong. "It's the Japanese," his wife said, her tone strained. "They have bombed the American base at Pearl Harbor." As fast as he could, Truman returned to the capital. Sadly, he listened as President Roosevelt spoke to a combined session of the Senate and the House of Representatives. "December 7, 1941 . . . a day that will live in infamy . . ." America was at war.

Immediately, there were some leaders in Washington who felt that Truman's committee should stop its investigations. Robert P. Patterson, an under-secretary of war, sent a letter to President Roosevelt: "It is in the public interest that the Committee should be suspended for the time being. It will impair our activities if we have to take time out to supply the Truman Committee all the information it desires." Expecting just such thinking, Truman had sent his own letter to the President three days earlier. In his letter, Truman promised to avoid any interference with military strategy or with military tactics.

"Keep doing your job," President Roosevelt told Truman.

With America at war, Truman pushed his committee to work even harder. Now it was not merely a matter of money being wasted. Lives were at stake, the lives of American servicemen and women. "If some fool contractor tries to pad his own pocket by building a cheaper building than promised or if some plant president starts turning out a rifle that doesn't meet standards, let's get 'em. And I mean get 'em good." Impressed with Truman's energy, one of his investigators nodded. "You would sure have made a tough soldier against those Germans on the battlefield." Truman's eyes flashed. "I already talked to the Army Chief of Staff about that. He says I'm too old. Tarnation, he's three years older than I am!"

But Harry proved that all soldiers do not have to carry guns. Wherever there was the slightest suspicion of mishandling of defense funds, Truman led an investigation.

Catching the Culprits

One morning, Harry stood with two other senators at a Texas airfield. On the surface, everything seemed to be rolling along smoothly at various construction sites. But the amounts listed for worker payrolls at the airport seemed incredibly high. "Do you want to see anything else?" the executive leading the tour asked the visiting senators. Truman paused, surveying all the structures nearby. "What's that under that hangar over there?" he asked. "Why, uh, it's just a gound-level basement," the guide answered, appearing somewhat nervous. "It's just used for storage. Now I think . . ." Truman stepped forward, moving in the direction of the hangar. "Fine. Raise up the trapdoor and let's see." It was easy to see that the executive did not want to grant Truman's request. It was even more obvious that Harry did not plan to go anywhere until the trapdoor was opened.

As the trapdoor swung open, the air was filled with the sound of voices. Slowly, men came walking out, their faces revealing their confusion. One hundred, 200, 300 . . . on and on they came. The mystery of the outrageous payroll was suddenly solved. Four hundred, 500, 600 . . . all of these men collecting wages for hiding, playing cards with friends, reading magazines. Truman was furious, his rage turning the air blue with every cussword he could think of. "This contractor will return every penny of overpayment for this job," Harry declared, "and I'll personally make sure he never gets another government contract!"

Such abuses incensed Truman. How could people swindle their own government, especially when the country was at war? Worse than that, there were those who endangered lives by building aircraft and firearms that did not meet safety standards. "It's murder," Truman told those at committee meetings. "It's plain and simple murder. And the murderers are not thugs off the street. They are supposedly law-abiding, respected citizens. Leaders of their communities. Men with sons of their own, doing these things that could possibly kill their own children."

MAKING HEADLINES

The more he saw what the Truman Committee was doing, the more President Roosevelt respected its chairman. From time to time, he would call Harry and invite him over to the White House. The Commander-in-Chief would pass along reports he received of possible problems in a munitions plant or arsenal. "Check on it," President Roosevelt would say. And Truman would do as he was ordered.

The Truman Committee staff grew in numbers – from five, to seven, then to nine. There was more work to be done all the time, and senators respected the effort. So did the entire country. Newspapers and radio stations carried stories about the results of investigations. But Truman made sure that each case was complete before reporters were called in. "We're not doing this job to make headlines," he told the committee and its staff.

But headlines were made, and Harry S. Truman became a familiar name to many Americans. As a result of the efforts of the Truman Committee, American taxpayers were saved an estimated $15 billion through the uncovering of waste and excess profits. It is impossible to know how many lives were saved, but estimates run in the thousands.

Although Harry was proud of his work with the Truman Committee, his daily efforts were a sad and constant reminder of how long the war was lasting. His memories of service in World War I remained vivid, yet America's involvement in it had been relatively short. As the casualty figures of the current war continued to stream in, the awareness of death and injury caused by the fighting touched him deeply. Families of Missouri soldiers found some comfort in notes from their own Senator Truman expressing his condolences.

Big Decisions

The war also took its toll on President Franklin Roosevelt. Despite the suffering and pain caused him by infantile paralysis long before becoming President, his early years in office seemed to provide new energy and vigor. But the years of commanding a momentous war effort had taken a heavy toll both physically and mentally.

First elected in 1932, then re-elected in 1936 and again in 1940, Roosevelt was the only man to have served three terms in the White House. Now, as 1944 dawned, people wondered if he would run again. *Could* he run again was the question many Democratic leaders asked among themselves. The old pep was gone, dark circles surrounded his eyes, his flesh coloring was pale. Nonetheless, the tired President decided to run one more time. After all, the country was at war. To step aside at such a time would be a form of desertion of duty.

The question of the candidate for Vice-President was debated long and loud among Democratic Party leaders. There was little doubt that President Roosevelt would win the election. But many also felt there was just as much certainty that he would not live through another four-year term. From the moment discussions opened as to who might be Roosevelt's running mate, Truman's name began popping up. "Everybody knows him from his work on the defense committee." "Yeah, but there's that old Pendergast connection." "Not much to look at, is he? Those thick glasses and all." "Are we talking about a vice-presidential candidate or a movie star?" "Isn't he kind of old?" "Sixty is all. Roosevelt is 61."

The arguments continued. As for Truman himself, he had no interest in being a vice-presidential candidate. He liked the Senate. He felt useful there. Anyway, he had his own choice for Vice-President. James Byrnes had been in the House of Representatives, the Senate, and had served on the Supreme Court. Now he was directing the Office of War Mobilization. Truman eagerly sought support for Byrnes.

But what really mattered was who President Roosevelt wanted as his running mate. It was clear he did not want his present Vice-President, Henry Wallace. But it seemed just as clear that although he respected what Truman had done for the Democratic Party and the country as a hard-working senator, Roosevelt had other people in mind. Constantly pestered by family and friends about his willingness to take the position, Truman shook his head. "No, I don't want to be Vice-President. But it doesn't really matter what *I* want anyway. It's what the President wants."

The matter was still up in the air when the Democrats held their convention in Chicago during July of 1944.

Regardless how the President felt, Henry Wallace wanted the vice-presidential nomination again. He worked busily to win support.

Truman went to the convention, too, but he did nothing about the vice-presidency. Instead, he directed his attention to helping write a strong party platform. During his free time, he enjoyed mingling with the delegates from Missouri.

"The Contrariest Missouri Mule"

On Wednesday of convention week, President Roosevelt easily won renomination to a fourth term of office. As politely as he could, Truman shook off questions as to whether he would be a vice-presidential candidate. But while sitting in a committee meeting, he was called to a nearby hotel room. One of his own chief backers, Bob Hannegan, held a telephone receiver. The voice on the other end was unmistakable. "Bob," President Roosevelt bellowed, "have you got that fellow lined up yet?" "No," Hannegan replied. "He is the contrariest Missouri mule I've ever dealt with."

Truman leaned forward, not wanting to miss a word. "Well," Roosevelt shouted again, "you tell him if he wants to break up the Democratic Party in the midst of a war, that's his responsibility!" Truman winced as President Roosevelt hung up. "Well, why didn't he tell me in the first place?" the surprised senator from Missouri asked.

To win the vice-presidential nomination, 589 delegate votes were needed. On the first round of voting, Henry Wallace got 429½ and Truman received 319½. While Harry calmly munched a hot dog in the Missouri delegation, his friend Bob Hannegan dashed around the convention floor trying to line up votes for Truman. Hannegan was effective. By the end of the second ballot, Harry won easily, receiving 1,031 votes.

A few weeks later, Truman had lunch with President

Roosevelt. "You'll have to do most of the campaigning for us," the haggard leader said, showing the strain of his office. Harry nodded, trying to hide his concern about the President's health. Afterwards, reporters surrounded him. "How does the President look?" one newsman shouted. "The President looked fine," Truman snapped back. "He ate a bigger meal than I did. He's as keen as a briar."

With that, Truman hurried away. He never did like lying to anyone.

Chapter 7
Dark Day in April

A hot September sun beat down on a crowd of people milling around the last car of the train. Suddenly the back door of the old combination sleeping and club car opened and a figure emerged. Shielding his bespectacled eyes with a raised hand, the gray-haired gentleman acknowledged the applause with a wide smile. "My name's Harry Truman, and I'm running for Vice-President of the United States with another fellow who is running for President of the United States." Glancing down, Truman rubbed his chin. "But I'll be doggoned if I can think of that other fella's name. Let's see . . ."

"Roosevelt, Harry!" someone called out. The crowd echoed the name, "Roosevelt!"

"That's it!" Truman laughed. "That's the ticket! And a winning ticket it will be!"

Across the country, the old train car rolled, with Truman constantly ready to speak. Most of his visits attracted large crowds. But when they didn't—as in the case of a little town in Idaho where only three retired schoolteachers showed up—Truman spoke anyway.

The Republican campaign was led by New York Governor Thomas Dewey. The mudslinging started early, and reporters hit Truman with a variety of sharp questions. "Is it true you have your wife on the office payroll, Senator Truman?" Harry nodded. "She earns her salary, too, every penny of it. I'm not aware of the woman making any mistake in her life, except for marrying me, of course!"

"Mr. Truman, is it true you went broke running a haberdashery?" "Yes, that's true enough. I think that experience helped me understand those folks in our country who are poor and need a helping hand."

"What about Tom Pendergast, Senator Truman? Wasn't he a friend of yours?" Harry's eyebrows went up. "Still is, as far as I'm concerned. And I hope he still will be when he gets out of prison."

"There's stories goin' around that you're a Jew, Mr. Truman. Is that so?" "No, it's not so," Harry snapped, "but if I were, I would not be ashamed of it."

Whatever question was asked, Truman had an answer. But it was the ugly rumors and gossip that he resented — whispers that President Roosevelt was sick and senile — that it was Bess Truman who really ran Harry's life simply because he affectionately called his wife "Boss."

"You Behave Yourself"

It was a nervous Franklin Roosevelt who listened to the election results on November 7, 1944. Not Harry, though. Surrounded by his Battery D buddies in Kansas City, he tickled the piano keys with his favorite selections. By 3:45 the next morning, Thomas Dewey threw in the towel. President Roosevelt had won an unprecedented fourth term, with Harry S. Truman as his Vice-President. They were inaugurated on January 20, 1945.

As soon as he could, Truman called his 91-year-old mother back in Grandview. "Did you hear all the ceremonies on the radio, Mama?" he asked. "Yes, Harry, I did. Now you listen to me a minute. You behave yourself up there," Martha Truman warned her new vice-presidential son with the tone of a mother just sending her child off to kindergarten. "You

*Shortly after the 1944 election, Harry S. Truman shares a
victory ride with President Franklin D. Roosevelt, winner of a
fourth consecutive term.* (Library of Congress.)

Ninety-one-year-old Martha Truman, Harry's mother, enjoys listening to the radio as her son receives the vice-presidential nomination at the Democratic National Convention in 1944. She died in 1947. (Library of Congress.)

behave yourself." Truman smiled. "I will, Mama," he promised.

Sooner than he had planned, Truman headed back to his home state of Missouri. Tom Pendergast died on January 26. Although his advisors cautioned Truman that it would not look good for him to attend the funeral, the warnings had no effect. "You say it wouldn't *look* good for me to show up there and I wouldn't feel right if I didn't," Truman declared. "I never did pay much attention to looks!"

Truman hoped to take some of the burdens off President Roosevelt, but it was not the chief executive's style of leadership to share much authority. At meetings with Prime Minister Winston Churchill of England and Premier Joseph Stalin of the Soviet Union, Roosevelt helped map the strategy aimed at bringing an end to World War II. He also helped structure a postwar organization whose goal would be to keep peace in the world. The purpose of this group, known as the United Nations, would be to gather and discuss international disagreements to prevent any future possibilities of war. Roosevelt's timetable was a busy one, often taking him out of Washington.

Truman's Darkest Day

Roosevelt's trip to Warm Springs, Georgia, in April of 1945 was planned to rebuild the leader's strength from the grueling war campaign that drained the man both physically and emotionally. The United States and its allies had crushed repeated attempts by the Germans and Japanese to regain momentum and achieve stability. World War II was grinding to an end, and, like everyone else in the nation, Harry S. Truman eagerly awaited that moment. As he left his Washington apartment the morning of April 12, 1945, he never dreamed that the next time he returned, he would be carrying the responsibilities of the presidency.

The death of Franklin Delano Roosevelt on the afternoon of April 12 plunged the country into a deep state of mourning. For 13 years he had led the nation, first out of economic depression and then through the pain and suffering of war. He was like a father, a familiar face in the newspaper and a comforting voice on the radio, forever offering hope and championing Americans to build on their strengths.

But who was this fellow who stood in his shadow—this unknown person from Missouri—Harry S. Truman? Oh, there were some who remembered him as being chairman of some defense committee. Of course, his cross-country jaunts on the railroad had won him some attention. But compared to Franklin Delano Roosevelt, Harry S. Truman appeared as a speck in the memories and minds of the nation's people. No one knew that more than the new President. He realized that as the war was winding down, he would have his own battle to wage—a battle to win the confidence and faith of the people in his own country as well as the people and leaders around the world.

DEADLY DECISIONS

The best way to win such a battle was to end the war. Quickly, Truman called together the leaders of all phases of American military operations. With a mind capable of soaking up and retaining enormous amounts of information, he frequently astounded his advisors. "The man's a machine!" one general remarked.

Truman would tolerate no underhandedness. Learning that the Russians were already violating promises made to the late President Roosevelt, Truman summoned Soviet Foreign Minister Molotov to a meeting. Not wasting words, Truman warned Molotov against any improper Russian behavior.

On May 1, 1945, Nazi chief Adolph Hitler committed

suicide. His successors sent out signs that they wanted peace. Truman could not have wished for a better birthday present on May 8 than victory in Europe. As he shared cake with Bess and Margaret, he learned the fighting in Europe was over. But the fighting with Japan still raged on.

In July, Truman traveled to Potsdam, Germany, a city near Berlin. He met with Churchill and Stalin to put together a peace treaty for Europe. Now that Germany had surrendered, decisions had to be made on supervising the country. It was while Truman was at Potsdam that he received a most unusual message.

"Babies satisfactorily born," the coded message read. Those three words spelled the beginning of the Atomic Age. The first atomic bomb had been exploded on July 16, 1945, at Alamogordo, New Mexico. Now a weapon, more devastating than any other in history, was available for use against the Japanese.

For Harry Truman, the decision whether or not to use the atomic bomb against the Japanese was not a difficult one to make. Leaders of the American military forces estimated that to attack Honshu, the main island of Japan, would cost 500,000 American lives. Japan would suffer similar losses, and another million on both sides would be maimed for the rest of their lives.

Although he was ready to order the dropping of atomic bombs, Truman wanted to give such a command only as a last resort. Scientists had provided him with staggering estimates of the deaths and destruction that would result. To drop an atomic bomb on a Japanese city would annihilate countless innocent citizens. Truman certainly did not want this to happen. Desperately, he issued an ultimatum to the Japanese demanding a complete, unconditional surrender. For hours the message was radioed into Japan, while millions of pamphlets urging surrender were dropped by daring airplane missions. Truman hoped and prayed the Japanese leaders would give up.

It was not to be. Not only was the American ultimatum ignored, Truman's demands for surrender were labeled "absurd." The Japanese did not give the slightest indication that they would give up under any conditions.

A Bloody End

His hopes for a peaceful surrender dashed, Truman gave the order to drop the first atomic bomb. It exploded over the Japanese military base of Hiroshima on August 6, 1945. The once busy and crowded city suddenly became a giant graveyard, with broken buildings standing like jagged tombstones among thousands of mangled, burned bodies. Still, the Japanese war leaders refused to surrender.

On August 9, a second atomic bomb was dropped, this one on the city of Nagasaki. Within hours came the request for surrender. Permission was asked that Emperor Hirohito retain his throne, a request that was quickly granted, and a cease fire went into effect on August 14. On September 2, 1945, General Douglas MacArthur supervised the Japanese surrender aboard the battleship *Missouri*.

"Bet you were proud it was the *Missouri* those papers were signed on," a reporter asked Truman shortly after news of the final surrender was announced. Stone-faced, the President shook his head. "It doesn't matter where this war ended. It's done, thank God. As for pride, I feel it for our people here at home and our friends overseas who fought and sacrificed many long years. We must always remember those who served with courage and pride who are not with us to share in this moment of silent guns. Now we must work to maintain a just and lasting peace with the same fervor and devotion that we have displayed in war."

TRUMAN'S "FAIR DEAL"

To back up his hopes for peace, Truman immediately sent to Congress 21 pieces of legislation that he considered necessary to restore the nation now that the war was over. Labeled "The Fair Deal," Truman's program included aid to education, a minimum wage increase, extended unemployment compensation, public and private housing, increased farm income, a plan for national health insurance, increased Social Security, and a program to guarantee equal job opportunities regardless of race or religion.

For a time after President Roosevelt's sudden death and while World War II was still going on, Congress and the media had treated Truman rather kindly. But with the introduction of "Fair Deal" policies, he was attacked from every corner. "The little man in the White House wants to remake the country," one senator blustered. "He needs reminding that nobody elected him as President." "Somebody needs to tell Mr. Truman that there doesn't need to be a law or policy for everything a person does in this country. We just got done fighting a war for freedom. Now let us enjoy it," another congressman declared.

The criticism stung Truman. No one was more aware than he that the people had not elected him as their President. He was surrounded by the team of advisors his predecessor had selected, and he knew he lacked the education, the culture, and the charisma of President Franklin Roosevelt.

Often Truman gained strength from his mother before her death in 1947. "A person's got lots of senses," Martha Truman told her son. "A person's got a sense of smell, a sense of hearing and seeing, and all the rest. But the most important sense a person has is common sense, and Harry, you've got more than your share of that. Just use it right and it will take you a long way."

THE "IRON CURTAIN" AND THE "COLD WAR"

His mother's words were comforting to Truman on many different occasions, as he dealt with domestic and international problems. Yet he sometimes wondered just how important common sense was in dealing with a calculating, determined power like the Soviet Union. Truman's counterpart in England, Winston Churchill, recognized the same devious traits in the Communist nation and coined a historic phrase when he visited Fulton, Missouri, in March of 1946 to receive an honorary degree. "From Stettin in the Baltic to Trieste in the Adriatic," Churchill declared, "an iron curtain has descended across the Continent."

The problems with the Soviet Union did not create an openly declared conflict like the bullets, bombs, and bloodshed of World War II. Rather, it was a cold war, a chilling, contrived program of taking over the governments of other countries to spread the doctrine of Communism. Truman knew that Stalin and the Soviet Union had to be kept constantly under surveillance.

FIGHTING THE UNIONS

Meanwhile, labor problems broke out on the home front when union leaders demanded increased wages and benefits. Gone was the unity, that patriotic spirit, so evident in the war years. Strikes erupted in oil, steel, coal mining, automobiles, aircraft, meat-packing, food—just about every industry imaginable. Like an angry bantam rooster, Truman challenged the union leaders to get their people back to work.

Many of these same leaders had openly backed Truman before, but when it was a question of friendship versus the welfare of the country, Truman removed friendship from his

England's Prime Minister Winston Churchill (left) and the
Soviet Union's Premier Joseph Stalin join hands with President
Truman during the Potsdam Conference in July of 1945.
(Harry S. Truman Library.)

mind. When Congress rejected his proposal to establish fact-finding boards to investigate each labor dispute, Truman set up a board of his own. "If you won't do the job that needs to be done," he told Congress, "I'll do it myself!"

The fight with the United Mine Workers was especially bitter, with crusty union president John L. Lewis defying every effort Truman made to end the coal miners' strike. "You'll not tell us what to do, Mr. Truman!" Lewis blustered through reporters. "It's not Mr. Truman telling you," came the curt White House answer. "It's the President of the United States!"

Truman knew that this particular strike would not only affect the United States, but also many other countries struggling to rebuild after the war and needing coal to do it. Nonetheless, the strong-willed Lewis would not give in, so Truman ordered the Department of the Interior to take over the mines. But when Lewis ordered a strike against the government, that was the last straw for Truman. He went into federal court to seek legal action. The court fined Lewis $10,000 and the United Mine Workers Union $3.5 million. The strike crumbled under the court ruling, but not before Lewis labeled Truman a "ruthless, heartless demigod."

PATTERNS FOR PEACE

Despite strong efforts by the United States and other nations to help those countries devastated during World War II, progress was slow. Western Europe recorded its worst winter on record in 1946–1947, followed by disastrously low grain crop yields. Moreover, European production of coal dropped, which led to a drastic reduction in industrial products.

By early 1947, it became evident that Greece and Turkey could easily succumb to Communism. Both nations had been weakened during the war and England, which had helped them financially, could no longer afford to do so.

The nation's First Family, President Harry S. Truman, wife Bess, and daughter Margaret, pose for a family portrait in the fall of 1946. (Library of Congress.)

On March 12, 1947, over nationwide radio, Truman declared, "It must be the policy of the United States to support free peoples who are resisting attempted subjugation by armed minorities or by outside pressures." He pledged a wide-sweeping and intense plan of economic and military aid for such countries. This plan was called "The Truman Doctrine."

As Truman wrestled with these problems, changes were also taking place in the field of communications. Radio had been the longtime voice to the people during the 20th century. On October 5, 1947, however, Truman made history when he delivered the first presidential address from the White House on television. "It's hard enough asking people to listen to me," Truman said, remembering the smooth, eloquent delivery of his predecessor, Franklin Roosevelt. "But knowing people are watching gives me little joy indeed. I'd put a bag over my head if I wasn't afraid someone would associate me with those no-good rats in the Ku Klux Klan."

The Marshall Plan

Few appointments were as wise and shrewd as when Truman tapped George C. Marshall to become secretary of state. A retired army general, Marshall displayed an immediate sense of what to do to rebuild those countries weakened by years of warfare. The Marshall Plan was based on a philosophy of "We will help you if you will help yourselves."

To those people who were starving, it was not enough just to provide food. That was only a temporary measure. The people needed to know how to grow their own. And if people were freezing, it was not enough just to provide coal. They needed to know how to mine their own. Certainly, money and goods were needed, but more importantly, people needed to know how to keep their lives and countries going after the money had been spent.

Despite the heavy emphasis on sharing advisors and providing new educational programs for industry and agriculture, the United States also needed to make a major financial investment in Europe. But the cost of financing the war had also strained American resources, and Truman knew it would be difficult to find the money needed to effectively apply the Marshall Plan.

One afternoon, in the Oval Office of the White House, Truman met with his old friend and leader of the House of Representatives, Sam Rayburn. Carefully, Truman laid out the proposed program to help bring Europe to its feet. "This is going to cost a lot of money, Mr. President," the astounded House leader said. "About 15 or 16 billion dollars," Truman replied, his voice remaining calm. Rayburn's eyes widened. "We can't afford it. It will bust the country." "Sam, that committee of mine saved that much with our investigations, and we were just going after waste. Now we're trying to save the world. If we don't help those people get on their feet again, we'll all go down the drain. If there's one thing I've learned in all the history books I've read, it's that our world is only as strong as the weakest country in it. Now, we've got some countries that are hurting bad. Let's help them."

Truman could be very convincing. Sam Rayburn was just one leader he won to the cause of the Marshall Plan. Others also joined in line. The necessary aid was approved by Congress and with steady, sure growth, Europe gradually regained its economic strength.

Now other matters began to occupy Harry's attention. As 1948 approached, speculation centered around the candidates for President. There was little doubt about who would be the Republican nominee. Perhaps Tom Dewey could not beat Franklin Roosevelt, but his supporters were sure he could trounce that "little man from Missouri." Although Truman waited to announce his intentions ("A little drama never hurt anybody," he sometimes said), he knew that he would run.

What Truman did from April 1945 until January 1949 was fill out Roosevelt's term. But he had ideas of his own, and he wanted to try them out. Still, he had made enemies, and winning the presidency on his own would be no easy task.

Chapter **8**

War—At Home and Abroad

Smiling at a crowd of Ohio voters, Truman shouted, "I've been told I'm a fool ridin' the back end of a train across the country. Some of my own staff people tell me I should just sit in front of a television camera and talk to you. Well, I tell you, when you go on television, they paint and powder your face, then they comb your hair and by that time I'd feel I was some kind of playactor." Pausing, Truman laughed. "I believe I'll leave that job to the movie folks—and the Republicans, of course! I'd rather just come out here, wrinkles and all, and we'll have a good talk."

"GIVE 'EM HELL, HARRY"

The crowd cheered and clapped. Truman took his campaign for the presidency to the people in 1948, and often he brought Bess (whom he still referred to as affectionately as "Boss") and daughter Margaret along with him. He traveled 32,000 miles, delivering over 700 speeches. He never seemed to wear out; when people gathered around him, they lifted his spirit and gave him new strength.

One day, during the campaign, a Montana cowhand rode a horse up to Truman and asked how old the animal was.

"Which end do you want me to look at, his tail or his mouth?" Truman answered, recalling those days when he helped his father in Independence. The cowhand laughed, "Why, he does know, doesn't he?" and rode off as the crowd cheered.

Another time, while he was speaking in a Seattle auditorium, Truman was ranting and raving against "Republicans who didn't know a squirrel from a skunk when one was sitting on their nose." From the balcony came a wild yell—"Give 'em hell, Harry! We'll take 'em!" With that, a new campaign slogan was born, a slogan Truman would hear from crowds wherever he traveled.

It was a hard-fought campaign, but not just against the Republicans. Former Vice-President Henry Wallace, declaring that Harry Truman would bring on a war with Russia, led a faction of the Democrats into the Progressive Party. Another Democratic faction backed South Carolina Governor Strom Thurmond, rebelling against a civil rights program endorsed by Harry and the Democratic Convention. Nicknamed "Dixiecrats," they officially called themselves The States' Rights Party.

The "Loser" Wins

By election day, the public opinion polls all agreed on one thing—Harry Truman was going to lose. They only disagreed on how much he would lose by. Even Truman's own staff members and friends held out little hope. As Tom Dewey busied himself writing an acceptance speech in New York City, Truman holed up in a small hotel room in Excelsior Springs, Missouri. He listened to a famous radio news announcer, H. V. Kaltenborn, commenting: "Mr. Truman is still ahead but these returns are from a few cities. When the returns come in from the country, the result will show Dewey winning overwhelmingly." Switching off the radio, Truman went to bed.

"Everyone makes mistakes!" Newly elected President Harry S. Truman enjoys a mighty laugh over the premature and incorrect edition of the Chicago Tribune *that announced his defeat in November of 1948. Sharing the joke is St. Louis Mayor Bernard Dickmann, a staunch Truman supporter.* (Harry S. Truman Library.)

The next thing he knew, Truman felt like he was in a topsy-turvy airplane. Then he put on his glasses and realized a Secret Service man was shaking him awake. Once again the radio was playing. "I don't see how Truman can be elected," Kaltenborn moaned, "but at this time he is winning by two million votes." "Not a bad lead, is it?" Truman asked the Secret Service man. "Not bad at all, Mr. President," came the answer.

It was many hours before the Republican candidate admitted that he had lost. When he was inaugurated on January 20, 1949, Truman could not help but feel a special pride. Ironically, the 80th Congress, which was controlled by Republicans, had provided funds for a grand celebration after the inauguration ceremonies. They had assumed Thomas Dewey would be the President. It gave Truman great satisfaction as he enjoyed the festivities.

But after the celebrating was over, Truman quickly settled into a busy routine. One thing was certain. He would not sacrifice the walk he took early each morning. "It clears my head and gets the blood pumping," he told the Secret Service guards who accompanied him. Many had to sprint to keep up with his pace.

The Buck Stops Here

One morning, Truman took a different route to get his two-mile walk in. As usual, his special guards followed behind as well as led the way. Over the Memorial Bridge they went, barely taking time to notice the smooth-flowing Potomac River.

Suddenly Truman spotted an open door. He peered in, noticed a stairway leading down and followed it. It was a frantic moment when Truman's guards realized they had lost the President! Soon they found the stairs and raced down to the bridge tender's room. Truman sat munching an apple. He smiled at his surprised guards.

"Sit down, boys, and rest your feet. I'm just finding out what Mr. Barnhill has to say about how the country is being run."

Truman always made time to listen to people. Whether it was Mr. Barnhill in Washington or a Mrs. Olson in Moline, Illinois, he listened to their complaints and compliments. Truman also read their letters and sent replies. "It's easy to shut yourself off in the White House. If you do, you don't know what people think and how they feel," Truman said. "Once you do that, you're in trouble. Sure, you're the boss in many ways. You give a lot of orders. But once you forget who the real boss is, the people, you start doing the job all wrong."

Harry was not afraid to make decisions. When he did, he took complete responsibility. A paperweight on his desk was engraved "The Buck Stops Here"; it served as a constant reminder to Harry that he must never try to pass blame onto anyone else. The President was the final voice of authority.

A President Reaches Out

Truman introduced program after program designed to help foreign nations rebuild themselves, thereby preventing the spread of Communism. In June 1948, when the Russians stopped all transportation between Berlin and West Germany, Soviet leaders hoped to force the entire German city to beg for help. "If we can't take food and supplies to those people in Berlin by land, we'll find another way," Truman promised. For almost a year, a fleet of airplanes, the Berlin Airlift, brought supplies to the cut-off Berliners. Finally, the Russians admitted defeat and reopened the land routes.

Truman also negotiated a pact between the United States, Canada, Iceland, and nine western European nations to fight Communist aggression in Europe. This military pact, called the North Atlantic Treaty Organization, or NATO, was approved by the Senate in July 1949. Then, in 1950, Truman introduced a plan to help the underdeveloped countries in Asia, Africa, South America, and the Middle East. Nicknamed "The Point Four Program," it was designed to help needy nations by providing American experts in such fields as agriculture and health.

CRISIS IN KOREA

Frustrated by the success of these American programs, the Soviet leaders decided to take their own kind of action. For years the Communists had controlled the people and land north of the 38th parallel in Korea. On June 24, 1950, North Korean forces invaded South Korea. Eager to gain more territory, North Korean leaders thought that Americans would not want to become involved in this little country on the other side of the world.

It was a foolish assumption, considering the philosophy and nature of Harry S. Truman. He called for an immediate meeting of the United Nations Security Council, requesting action against the invasion by North Korean troops. The attending members voted 9–0 that fighting in Korea should cease and that the North Korean forces should leave South Korea at once. Peace-keeping UN soldiers were ordered to the country. Because the Russians did not attend the Security Council meeting, they could not veto the council's action. (Never again did the Soviet Union miss a meeting of the Security Council when one was called.)

American civilians were ordered out of South Korea, and General Douglas MacArthur, the top U.S. military leader in the area, was ordered in to take charge. It was hoped the South Korean forces of President Syngman Rhee could turn back the invaders. That way no American troops would be involved. It was not to be that simple, however, because Rhee's South Korean forces were no match against the North Korean attackers. MacArthur sent word that American military forces were needed, and Truman had to decide whether or not to send troops.

Carefully Truman pondered his choices. He knew that Korea was of little military and economic importance to the United States. Most Americans did not even know where the country was. Certainly Syngman Rhee was no great pillar of democracy. Again and again, he had resisted efforts to make South Korea a more democratic nation. Critics of his government often found themselves prisoners.

Yet Truman realized that whatever decision he made, it could not be based on how well known Korea was or the political stand of its president. A small country had been deliberately attacked by Communist forces. Help was needed. If not stopped in Korea, how many other countries would the Communists invade?

Entering the Battle

His decision made, Truman wired General MacArthur to deploy whatever American forces he needed to turn back the invaders. A shrewd and skilled battle technician, the general went right to work. He hoped to end the fighting swiftly.

But it was not swift enough for some Americans. When the fighting continued for weeks, then months, some in the United States Senate criticized Truman for involving the country in the Korean conflict. "It is simply not our war!" one senator thundered. "President Truman would have the United States patrolling the entire world. We are not patrol boys!" Reading the account of the speech in a newspaper, Truman snapped, "No, but we are watchdogs against those creeping Communists!"

Through wise planning and strategy, MacArthur soon cleared South Korea of the invaders. Wanting to convince the North Koreans they were beaten and that further aggression would not pay, Truman ordered MacArthur to negotiate a surrender.

It was then that another problem arose. Mao Tse-Tung, leader of Red China, declared that his country "will not stand idly by and see North Korea invaded."

It was an ominous warning, one that Truman pondered carefully. He sent word to MacArthur to try everything possible to secure a peaceful surrender. Twice the general tried, but no surrender came. MacArthur then ordered his troops into North Korea.

In October 1950, Truman met with General MacArthur. They talked about rebuilding Korea after the conflict and establishing a military organization in the Pacific area similar to the NATO organization in the Atlantic. As to any intervention by the Red Chinese, or possibly even the Soviets, in defense of the Communist forces in North Korea, MacArthur shook his head. He promised Truman that his troops could get the job done in six weeks. It looked like there would be much to be thankful for at Thanksgiving.

At first, everything went smoothly. MacArthur's soldiers swept into North Korea, soon capturing its capital city. However, when Red Chinese soldiers began turning up among the prisoners, Truman was troubled. Would Mao Tse-Tung order his country's soldiers into Korea for a full-scale attack?

Truman's worries increased with news that Communist planes from Manchuria were attacking the United Nations troops. MacArthur requested permission to pursue such planes and bomb Chinese ground targets. Truman carefully studied the situation. To grant MacArthur's request surely would bring

Red China into the conflict. Such warfare would fall right into the hands of the Soviet Union. Russian leaders would enjoy watching the United States and China weaken themselves by fighting.

The cheerful Thanksgiving Truman had hoped for crumbled. Christmas was equally glum. In Korea, North Korean and United Nations forces moved back and forth, each side winning ground and then giving it up again. MacArthur wanted more power, the right to bomb Chinese supply bases and chase enemy planes into China. Meeting with his military advisors, Truman heard another opinion–"Do not attack China." Truman felt the same way. With the utmost care, he set in motion plans for a cease-fire in Korea. Now that the enemy invaders were out of South Korea, it could be an honorable peace treaty.

But while Truman was preparing to negotiate a treaty, General MacArthur complicated the efforts for peace. Feeling that Truman was resisting any aggressive actions because of concern for his own personal political popularity, MacArthur began speaking out to reporters. The military commander advocated blockading the Chinese coast and bombing Chinese industrial centers.

Firing a Hero

Truman was greatly disturbed by General MacArthur's statements. It was not merely that they conflicted with his own, but the general was taking his case to the public and the press before going to his commander-in-chief. "If there is one thing this man should understand," Truman told his advisors, "it is the line of authority, the chain of command."

Harry sent word to MacArthur to stop making public statements before sharing them first with his superiors. But the general did not see Truman as a superior in this matter. "There are matters that only military leaders can understand,"

Truly a Man of Letters

No United States President wrote more letters than Harry S. Truman. It was a habit carried over from the early days in Missouri. Historians estimate that Truman wrote over 100,000 letters in his lifetime.

Unlike many elected officials, Truman made sure no public money ever went for personal letters he sent. One morning his secretary found three pennies on her desk when she arrived at work. When she asked President Truman about the money, he smiled. ''I was writing a letter home to my mother,'' he replied. ''I needed to borrow one of your stamps.''

Truman did not send every letter he wrote. He thought letter-writing was the best way of keeping in contact with relatives and friends. But he also believed it was good therapy for getting rid of anger. Whenever he became disgusted with someone, he poured out his feelings on paper. Then he simply put the letter in a desk drawer or folder.

But there was one such letter that Truman did send. It caused more of a public outcry than any other.

Daughter Margaret was actively pursuing a singing career. In December of 1950, she gave the final concert of an arranged tour at Constitution Hall in Washington, D.C. It was a sad and tired Harry Truman who attended the concert that evening. American soldiers were fighting in Korea, and there was no end in sight. That afternoon, his friend since boyhood who was also his press secretary, Charlie Ross, had died of a heart attack.

Arising at daybreak the next morning, Truman read a review of Margaret's concert in the *Washington Post*. ''She is flat a good deal of the time,'' wrote the critic, Paul Hume. ''She communicates nothing of the music she presents.''

Truman reached for a pen and wrote a letter. If Hume's review was hot, Truman's answer to it was scalding. Harry told the reviewer he sounded like ''a frustrated man that never made a success, an eight-ulcer man on a four-ulcer job and all four ulcers working.''

Although Truman's note was not intended for publication, Hume did just that. It was clearly an effort to embarrass the President of the United States. But Truman was *not* embarrassed. ''I did not write the letter as the President,'' he asserted. ''I wrote it as a human being.''

Sadly enough, Truman's own advisors thought he should not have sent the letter to Paul Hume. They thought it lowered the dignity of the presidency. ''It will only cause you trouble,'' his aides insisted. ''Wait until *we* start getting mail about this.'' Truman shook his head. ''I'll bet about 80 percent are on my side.''

Then the letters poured in. ''I wouldn't have written a letter,'' one man said. ''I'd have pounded the guy over the head.'' Another woman wrote, ''I would hope my hus-

band would have defended our daughter the
way you defended yours.''
     The letters for and against were finally
counted. A total of 81 percent supported
Truman and his letter. ''You just don't
understand human nature,'' Truman told his
advisors.
     Clearly, Harry S. Truman did!

MacArthur said later. "President Truman had neither the background nor the grasp of the Korean and Chinese situation."

Whether Truman lacked the experience or the understanding was debated then and has been debated since. However, one point remained clear. He had the power to relieve General MacArthur from duty. When the military leader issued a statement on March 30, 1951, threatening to take the fighting into China's coastal areas and interior bases, Truman was enraged. "Why, this man even demands that North Korea surrender to him personally!" Truman fumed to his advisors. "I've had all I care to have of General Douglas MacArthur!"

Truman held no personal feelings against MacArthur. During the early stages of the Korean conflict, no one had praised the World War II hero more. Harry had called MacArthur's actions "brilliant" and "noble." Even when the general miscalculated enemy strength and misread their intentions, Truman stood solidly behind MacArthur. But the constant attempts to undermine Harry's authority was in direct violation of the Constitution of the United States. The "buck" stopped with the power of the President, the commander of the military forces, and head of civilian activities in the executive branch of the government.

In April 1951 came the last straw in the Harry Truman-Douglas MacArthur feud. A letter written by the general was read openly on the floor of the House of Representatives. MacArthur called for increased fighting with the help of Chiang Kai-shek's forces. The general went on to predict ". . . .that if we lose this war to Communism in Asia the fall of Europe is inevitable; win it and Europe most probably would avoid war and yet preserve freedom."

"I can tolerate a man's mistakes in thinking," Truman told his advisors, "but I cannot tolerate complete disobedience." On April 11, 1951, Truman released the following statement:

> With deep regret, I have concluded that General of the Army Douglas MacArthur is unable to give his wholehearted support to the policies of the United States government and of the United Nations in matters pertaining to his official duties. In view of the specific responsibilities imposed upon me by the Constitution of the United States and the added responsibility which has been entrusted to me by the United Nations, I have decided that I must make a change of command in the Far East. I have, therefore, relieved General MacArthur of his commands and have designated Lieutenant General Matthew B. Ridgeway as his successor.

Truman's action dismissing MacArthur exploded louder than a bomb. Americans were outraged in behalf of their hero general; 78,000 letters and telegrams flooded the White House. Senators and representatives called for Truman's resignation, some even threatening impeachment. The Gallup opinion poll reported only 29% of Americans supported the dismissal.

General MacArthur's return to the United States raised the level of the outcry. Hundreds of thousands cheered him in parades. He spoke before a combined session of the Senate and House of Representatives. He recalled an old song sung at West Point when he was a cadet that "proclaimed most proudly that old soldiers never die, they just fade away . . . I now close my military career and just fade away, an old soldier who tried to do his duty as God gave him the light to see that duty. Goodbye."

Truman had little use for MacArthur's farewells. As President, he did not even object to congressional committees asking MacArthur to testify as to why he was dismissed. He testified for three days, while other witnesses also made statements. At the end of seven weeks, MacArthur emerged from the hearings appearing ambitious, arrogant, vain, and boring. Support for Harry immediately increased, with many Americans agreeing that MacArthur's dismissal had been necessary.

A Surprise Announcement

Most Democratic leaders were sure that Truman would run for re-election in 1952. Surely anyone who could weather a storm of protest like the one that erupted after General MacArthur's dismissal could tackle another four years in the White House. But at a dinner in Washington, in the spring, Truman made a surprise announcement.

"I shall not be a candidate for re-election." He smiled a moment, stealing a glance at Bess. "I have served my country long, and I think efficiently and honestly. I shall not accept renomination."

It was done. Over. And anyone who knew Harry S. Truman at all knew better than to argue his decision with him.

Chapter 9
Final Duties

President Harry Truman, fresh from a brisk morning walk, sat at his White House desk thinking about the day ahead of him—a day filled with documents to read, scheduled meetings, and a speech to write for later in the week. On the other side of the world, the Korean conflict continued, its ever-increasing casualty figures and financial drain dampening the spirits of Americans. At home, a steel strike added to the economic crisis. It was not a cheerful time for the President of the United States, and Truman felt weighted down by the moment in office.

Fully aware that the end of his term was in sight—that now he was, in political terms, "a lame duck," he took pen in hand and made out a list of the duties of the President. Always the scholar of history, Truman felt the need to reflect on his position while thinking about a suitable candidate within the Democratic Party who might take his place. There was never any doubt concerning Truman's devotion to his party. Truman wrote:

1. By the Constitution, he is the chief executive of the government.
2. By the Constitution, he is commander-in-chief of the armed forces.
3. By the Constitution, he is the responsible head of foreign

Always glad to relax at the keyboard, President Harry S. Truman accompanies some of his political colleagues at a National Press Club dinner held in Washington in 1951. (Library of Congress.)

policy and, with the help of his secretary of state, implements foreign policy.

4. He is the leader of his party, makes and carries out party platform as best he can.

5. He is the social head of the state. He entertains visiting heads of state.

6. He is the number-one public relations man of the government. He spends a lot of time persuading people to do what they should do without persuasion.

7. He has more duties and powers than a Roman emperor, a general, a Hitler, or a Mussolini; but he never uses those

powers or prerogatives, because he is a democrat (with a little "d") and believes in the Magna Carta and the Bill of Rights. But first he believes in the XXth chapter of Exodus, the Vth chapter of Deuteronomy, and the V, VI, and VIIth chapters of the Gospel according to St. Matthew.
8. He should be a Cincinnatus, Marcus Aurelius Antoninus, a Cato, Washington, Jefferson, and Jackson all in one. I fear that there is no such man. But if we have one who tries to do right because it is right, the greatest republic in the history of the world will survive.

While fulfilling the responsibilities of the presidency early in the election year of 1952, Truman played an active role within the Democratic Party. He assumed the Republican nomination would go to Ohio Senator Robert Taft, who would be "easy pickings" for any Democratic candidate. Taft, the son of a former President, had built up a solid following among fellow Republicans, but he lacked any personal warmth that would be attractive to the American people.

Truman's first choice for the Democratic nomination was Governor Adlai Stevenson of Illinois, whose own family also had figured in the nation's history. (His grandfather had served a term as Vice-President in the second presidency of Grover Cleveland.) Governor Stevenson proved a frustration to Truman because he could not make up his mind whether to run for leader of his state or of his country. In the meantime, Truman was persuaded to lend support to his own Vice-President, Alben Barkley of Kentucky, who, at 74, would have been the oldest President to be elected. But Stevenson eventually decided to run, seeking and winning the support of the party faithful, including Harry S. Truman.

Stevenson's opponent did not turn out to be Taft, however. Instead, it was General Dwight D. Eisenhower, who had only declared his party affiliation as a Republican in January of 1952. Truman used Eisenhower's indecision effectively in his campaign speeches for Stevenson. "I'm still not sure he's Republican or Democrat," the chief executive growled. "I do know this as a student of history. A good general does not always make a good President!" But the more Truman traveled and spoke, the more aware he became that "Ike" had very few enemies.

UNDER ATTACK

By contrast, there were many times in 1952 when Truman felt he had nothing *but* enemies. A truce in the Korean fighting seemed always just beyond reach. And when a steel strike jeopardized the production of weapons needed overseas, Truman ordered the government to step in and take over the companies. "Unconstitutional!" charged steel industry officials, and the United States Supreme Court backed them up. When Congress passed legislation giving oil deposits below the sea to southern oil states, Truman promptly vetoed the measure. "All the benefits go to just a few states at the expense of the rest," he asserted. "Then we'll just vote Republican this year and see how you like that!" replied angry political leaders from the South.

The "Truman Scandals"

The Republicans were quick to take advantage of any possible opportunities to attack the Truman administration. When a number of low-level government officials were found guilty of taking bribes, failing to file taxes, and accepting questionable gifts, rumors flew that the entire government was corrupt.

Once more the Pendergast name was brought up, with insinuations and outright accusations that Truman had climbed his way to the presidency with the assistance of political machinery oiled with corruption and underhanded tactics. "Not so!" Truman bristled. "I stand for honest government and I have worked for it all my life!" Although Truman fired all those found guilty of any illegal actions, the label "Truman Scandals" lingered, tainting the images of Democratic candidates at the national, state, and local levels.

Truman got in his share of offensive fighting too, making scathing attacks on Republican Senator Joseph McCarthy, who had loosely charged countless government workers with being Communists or having Communist associations. Another Republican senator called General George Marshall a front man for traitors, and vice-presidential candidate Richard Nixon had labeled Truman himself "a traitor." Truman shook his head. "If George Marshall and I are traitors," he thundered to audiences, "then this country is in a helluva fix."

On November 4, 1952, the voters of the nation went to the polls. Eisenhower took an early lead which increased steadily as the votes were tallied. The final count revealed that Adlai Stevenson had lost by over six million votes.

Eager to head home to Independence, Truman urged Bess to start packing their bags. Before leaving, however, the chief executive invited his successor to the White House, where President-elect Eisenhower was given briefing sessions. Truman had his aides do the same with their successors.

"JUST CALL ME HARRY!"

Shortly before noon on Tuesday, January 20, 1953, Harry S. Truman witnessed the swearing in of President Dwight D. Eisenhower by Chief Justice Fred Vinson, a Truman appointee. After enjoying a lunch with old friends, the now former President and his wife headed for the railroad station and boarded a train.

However, if Truman thought he was going to slip silently

out of the city, he was very mistaken. A cheering crowd of 5,000 people gathered to bid their past leader a grateful farewell. "Thanks, President Truman!" one onlooker yelled out. A smiling Harry Truman waved. "Not President Truman," he hollered back. "Just Mr. Truman. Better yet, just call me Harry."

And then it was over. As the train rolled out of the Washington station and headed west, it left behind the memories of countless meetings, budgets, interviews, decisions, and all the rest that goes with holding the highest office in the nation. Harry Truman slipped off his glasses, leaned his head back, and listened to the steady beat of the metal wheels rolling against the track.

Another 10,000 people stood waiting in the Independence station to welcome their mighty man from Missouri. Still another 5,000 lined the neighborhood pathways around the Truman family home on Delaware Street. Overcome with the warmth and devotion shown, both Harry and Bess Truman fought to hold back their tears.

A "Simple Man"

It was good to be back home in Independence, out of the public spotlight and away from the frantic pace of the nation's capital. "I'm basically a simple man with simple tastes," Truman told a visiting reporter during an interview in April of 1953. He did not miss the elaborate state dinners with servants constantly at his elbow and grand china and silverware in front of him on the table. He much preferred a soft-boiled egg at breakfast, a sandwich for lunch, and roast beef with potatoes for supper. The days of bourbon and water passed away also, replaced with hearty iced tea. Truman enjoyed working at a Kansas City office in the daytime and sharing the evenings quietly with Bess and relatives.

A gall bladder attack and operation slowed Truman

briefly in 1954, but soon he was walking and working again. With studied care and diligence, he assembled his memoirs, recognizing that the part he played in history would be of major interest in the years to come. Published in 1955 and 1956, the two volumes found an eager reading audience. At the rate of 10 copies a minute, Truman signed 4,000 volumes at his first autograph party.

Father of the Bride — and Library

In April of 1956, Truman played a role completely new to him as he proudly escorted his daughter Margaret down the main aisle of Trinity Episcopal Church in Independence. She married E. Clifton Daniel, Jr., a well-known New York newspaper executive. "A beautiful bride, don't you think?" Truman asked the assembled reporters covering the event. "Thank goodness she got her mother's looks!"

Truman next turned his full attention to the construction of the presidential library to be built in his honor. At first he openly opposed the modern design of the one-story, half circular building, but gradually he came to appreciate its efficient use of space and its attractive appearance. He was especially delighted with the plans for a private office in the rear where he could work at any time.

Not satisfied merely helping with the library plans, Truman actively joined in the effort to raise funds. Donations poured in from people who were once again happy to hear the former first executive speak. "You probably thought, or maybe you hoped, you had heard the last from me when I left office," Truman told the audiences who gathered to hear him speak. "Well, once we get this library built, maybe then I'll shut up."

Thanks to Truman's personal efforts at every stage, the library plans and construction ran ahead of schedule. In July of 1957, official dedication ceremonies were held for the Harry

After leaving the presidency, Truman proved an able, perceptive recorder of the experiences and events during his years in office. (Harry S. Truman Library.)

S. Truman Library in Independence. Guest speaker for the event was Eleanor Roosevelt. "It is most appropriate that this library be built but a few blocks from the Truman family home," the former First Lady observed, "as I am quite certain that Harry S. Truman will use its facilities more than anyone else." Mrs. Roosevelt could not have been more right. Each day the former President made the quick walk to the library, where he spent much of his time answering letters from people all over the world.

One afternoon a junior high school history teacher frantically raced around the Truman Library looking for five students who had disappeared from the class she had brought on a field trip. It was with relief and considerable embarrassment that she found her students sitting in Truman's private office chambers. Before the teacher could apologize or explain, Truman silenced her with a hand motion and said, "We were all just talking about this grand country of ours. I get kind of windy about the topic, like most politicians do, and the time just slipped away from us."

Nothing gave Harry Truman a bigger thrill than talking to young people about their country and their government. "Know the place where you live," he counseled them, "and find out who runs your city and state government. Learn how laws are made and get involved. Read about the people who made this country great because they deserve to be remembered for their contributions. Not only that, maybe the deeds of others will inspire you to set a few special goals for yourself."

A Politician to the End

Although Truman worked hard to maintain a private life in Independence, he could never turn down an invitation to attend the National Democratic Conventions held every four years. It was a chance to meet again with old friends, share stories of the past, and lift the crowd to its feet with a spirited speech. Again, when "Give 'em hell, Harry!" thundered across the vast convention halls, that is just what he did.

There was also no arm-twisting needed to enjoy the role of grandfather. Daughter Margaret gave birth to four boys — Clifton, William, Harrison, and Thomas — over the years, and Grandfather Truman frequently admonished Bess "not to spoil those boys." He then proceeded to do just that.

In 1960 the Democrats regained the presidency, replacing outgoing Dwight Eisenhower with the youngest man ever to hold the position — John Fitzgerald Kennedy. The new President had not been Truman's first choice — he had preferred Lyndon Baines Johnson, who subsequently accepted the vice-presidential spot. Yet Kennedy soon won the admiration and respect of Truman, and the two men conferred on a variety of topics. Kennedy's assassination on November 22, 1963, was a stunning blow to the aging Truman.

In 1964, President Lyndon Baines Johnson flew to Independence, where he officially signed the Medicare Bill on the stage of the Truman Library auditorium. Recalling Truman's efforts to legislate a national health program almost 20 years before, Johnson noted, "It has taken us awhile to get the job done, sir, and I'm sorry we kept you waiting." Harry smiled. "Well, now that we've got a bill to take care of us older folks, I might start getting there myself."

Though spoken in jest, the words turned prophetic. Late in the year, he took a fall in his bathroom and never fully regained his strength. A cane helped give the more than 80-year-old man his balance, but there could be no more jaunty morning walks and the visits to the library ceased. Gradually, Truman lost weight, and soon his vision and hearing also began to slip away.

On December 26, 1972, Harry S. Truman died in a Kansas City hospital, at the age of 88. He was buried near

Assassination—A Constant Shadow Over the Presidency

Everyone recognizes the power and importance of being President of the United States. Yet few people consider the danger of being the nation's top elected official. Bullets of assassins have cut down four chief executives —Abraham Lincoln in 1865, James Garfield in 1881, William McKinley in 1901, and John Kennedy in 1963. On the afternoon of November 1, 1950, the intended victim for assassination was Harry S. Truman.

The Truman family had been living in Blair House while the White House across the street was being repaired. At four o'clock in the afternoon, Truman was scheduled to dedicate a statue at Arlington National Cemetery. He decided to take a nap in the second-floor bedroom.

If they had had their way, Griselio Torresola and Oscar Collazo would have made certain Truman never awakened. The two Puerto Rican Nationalists approached Blair House at about 2:30. They were well-armed and carried plenty of ammunition. After recognizing Puerto Rico as a commonwealth, Truman had recently appointed its first governor. Torresola and Collazo wanted the country to be totally independent. By killing President Truman, the two men were sure the United States government would be thrown into turmoil. In all the confusion, the Puerto Rican Nationalists could declare their country free.

It was a wild plan. Torresola and Collazo

knew they had to get past trained White House Guards. The two men approached the entrance to Blair House cautiously. As they started up the front steps, two guards blocked their way and began asking questions. Torresola and Collazo opened fire. The gunshots crackled in the afternoon air, waking Truman and bringing him to the bedroom window. "Get back!" a guard shouted, and the President did just that.

In the space of three minutes, 31 gunshots were exchanged. By the time it was over, Torresola and a White House guard, Leslie Coffelt, lay dead. Collazo and two additional White House guards were injured.

Harry Truman went on to keep his appointment at Arlington National Cemetery. He made no mention of the events that took place earlier in the afternoon.

When asked about the danger of possible assassination, Truman's answers were quick and direct. "A President has to expect such things," he explained. "If someone wants to shoot you, he'll probably do it and nothing can help you out. It's an ongoing risk that goes with the job."

Every effort is made to keep the President of the United States safe from harm. Yet there is always a danger. When President John Kennedy was assassinated, reporters immediately sought statements from past chief executives. Former Presidents Herbert Hoover and Dwight Eisenhower both expressed feelings of "shock" and "deep loss."

No statement came from Truman. Too grief-stricken to speak, the saddened old man simply went off to bed.

the library which bears his name and which filled him with such pleasure and pride after the years of his presidency.

"I'd like to be remembered as an ordinary man called to do an extraordinary job," Harry S. Truman had said once.

Indeed, the presidency of the United States is an "extraordinary job."

But there was little about Harry S. Truman that was ordinary.

Chapter 10

The Legacy of the Truman Presidency

Periodically, historians are surveyed as to their evaluations of those men who have served as President of the United States. In most surveys, the quality of a President's leadership is carefully scrutinized based on his ability to effectively deal with the events and situations that took place within his term or terms of office. The Presidents are then labeled as great, near great, average, below average, or failure. In the vast majority of such evaluational surveys, Harry S. Truman places in the top 10 of American Presidents, usually being given a "near great" rating.

Why? What was it about this bespectacled, fiesty fellow from Independence, Missouri, that allowed him to capture such an esteemed position among America's chief executives? He could hardly boast any of the educational and cultural credentials of others who occupied the same office before and after him. On the physical side of the ledger, he was no superman, being afflicted with weak vision all his life. And at times, the loyalty he felt for friends and associates could allow his usually correct judgment to become clouded.

His desire to be as knowledgeable as possible in every area led him to make decisions he eventually came to regret. The establishment of the Central Intelligence Agency in 1947 was one such example. Truman started the CIA for the purpose of compiling and condensing the information sent in from intelligence bureaus all over the world. In such a framework, the President "would get *one* report on what was going on in various parts of the world." Truman lived to regret setting up the agency, expressing alarm that "those fellows in the CIA don't just report on wars and the like, they go out and make their own, and there's nobody to keep track of what they're up to."

Certainly, Truman's snappy, overly dramatic retorts to reporters' questions managed to make molehills into mountains at times. Often he stirred up unnecessary controversy and needless arguments with differing individuals and factions.

Why, then, would Harry S. Truman rank among the greatest Presidents of the United States?

A "People's President"

Perhaps many of his strengths as a President have to do with his inner character. Growing up in the heartland of America, young Harry Truman came to know the horse-and-buggy days of 19th-century Missouri. He watched his father and mother struggle to make a living in farming and animal trading; then he joined the struggle himself. Books offered a special joy, the excitement of words, a new world.

From the moment he organized the publication of a high school newspaper in Independence, at the turn of the century, Truman displayed a unique talent for administration. Such skills served him well on the battlefields of France during World War I, but they were not enough to provide him financial success as an investor and businessman. Finding a real home in the political arena during the mid-1920s, Truman focused his total attention on people and their needs. It was the foundation of his entire public career and guided his private life as well.

Harry S. Truman managed to develop a broad, sweeping understanding of men, women, and children in all parts of the world. This unusual perception allowed him to deal cautiously with leaders who would use their power negatively, and openly with leaders who shared the humanitarian concerns he felt deeply. He could communicate with the man on the street as comfortably as he could with a king or prime minister.

Although Truman understood the respect due visiting dignitaries, he refused to be intimidated by unfair demands or biased complaints. "Truman was capable of not only hearing what people were saying as they spoke," observed the longtime government official Averell Harriman, "but he could instantly analyze why they were saying what they were and the consequences for the future."

Good Neighbor to the World

At the end of World War II, it would not have been surprising if the American people had chosen to withdraw into their own national boundaries. The physical, emotional, and financial strains placed upon people at war often contribute to a feeling of wanting to be isolated after the war is over.

Recognizing that the United States could no longer isolate itself from the rest of the world, one of Truman's first decisions after taking office was to attend the opening ceremonies of the United Nations and sign the charter of that organization. With this act, Truman pledged the support of the United States to work for peace everywhere in the world.

The signing of the UN Charter on June 26, 1945, was only the first of many actions that Harry Truman took to show the world his commitment to life, liberty, and the pursuit of happiness for every living person on earth. As soon as the guns of World War II were stilled, he initiated his own "Fair Deal" programs to improve the lives of American citizens. Through the Truman Doctrine, he showed all nations that the

United States heard the sounds of the world's poor and oppressed—and stood ready to help. The Truman Doctrine was expanded through the Marshall Plan, a plan not only to provide immediate aid and assistance to countries in need, but to plant seeds of recovery for the future through education and technology.

An Undaunted Leader

Throughout his presidency, Truman was subjected to constant criticism and attempted intimidation by leaders of the Communist nations, yet he pursued his policies undaunted. The Berlin airlift illustrated his shrewdness and courage while also demonstrating America's desire to assist those in need. Then, to prevent further such reoccurrences, Truman helped establish the North Atlantic Treaty Organization (NATO).

When the Communists chose to make a direct offensive attack in the 1950 Korean conflict, Truman sent a clear message that America stood ready to meet force with force. After developing so many active programs of a peaceful nature around the world, the strong, aggressive action of Truman during the Korean conflict was a dramatic contrast. Yet this action underscored America's total commitment to world peace, even when the cost in lives and finances was staggering.

There are many who have said that if Franklin Delano Roosevelt had completed his fourth term in office, Harry S. Truman might have merely been numbered among so many soon-forgotten Vice-Presidents. There are others who argue that after Roosevelt had stepped down, Truman undoubtedly would have run for the presidency on his own and would have won. Such speculation may prove fascinating for history buffs, but the fact remains that on an April afternoon in 1945, the death of President Franklin Delano Roosevelt thrust Harry S. Truman front and center onto the stage of destiny. His character as a man and his leadership as a President combined to leave an indelible mark on the pages of history.

Bibliography

Collins, David R. *Harry S. Truman.* Champaign, Illinois: Garrard Publishing Company, 1975. This easy-to-read biography highlights the public and personal life of the 33rd President.

Daniels, Jonathan. *The Man from Independence.* Philadelphia: Lippincott, 1950. A detailed account of the life of Harry S. Truman that begins with his childhood days in Missouri and follows him into the presidency of the United States.

Ferrell, Robert H. *Truman.* New York: Viking, 1984. This smooth-flowing biography was compiled as a special tribute to Harry S. Truman on the anniversary of the 100th year of his birth. This "centenary remembrance" is a fascinating combination of words and pictures.

Gies, Joseph. *Harry S. Truman—A Pictorial Biography.* Garden City: Doubleday and Company, 1968. This photo scrapbook captures the major events and many moods of the 33rd President.

Miller, Merle. *Plain Speaking.* New York: G. P. Putnam's Sons, 1973. With Miller serving as questioner, Harry S. Truman, his relatives, and his associates reveal their attitudes and feelings. This oral biography offers a unique look at the subject through his own words.

Richards, Kenneth G. *Harry S. Truman.* Chicago: Children's Press, 1968. This book is part of a humanities series entitled "People of Destiny." Although biographical data are included, the major thrust of the volume is to establish Harry S. Truman as a contributor to the betterment of people.

Robbins, Jhan. *Bess and Harry.* New York: G. P. Putnam's Sons, 1980. This book reveals much of the character of the 33rd President and his wife.

Steinberg, Alfred. *Harry S. Truman.* New York: G. P. Putnam's Sons, 1963. This biography, aimed at junior-senior high readers, is rich with personal anecdotes. Complicated events are made simple without diluting the facts.

Truman, Harry S. *Year of Decision.* New York: Doubleday, 1955. *Years of Trial and Hope.* New York: Doubleday, 1956. These two books spotlight the years of Harry S. Truman's presidency through the perspective of the man who lived through them.

Truman, Margaret. *Harry S. Truman.* New York: William Morrow & Company, 1973. With the skill of a sensitive biographer and the love of a devoted daughter, Margaret Truman traces her father's personal and public life. Her unique position in his life provides readers with a countless collection of priceless anecdotes that enrich this portrait of an extraordinary man.

Index